The Arms Export Challenge

Brookings Occasional Papers

The Arms Export Challenge

Cooperative Approaches to Export Management and Defense Conversion

KEVIN O'PREY

THE BROOKINGS INSTITUTION
Washington, D.C.

Brookings Occasional Papers

THE BROOKINGS INSTITUTION is a private nonprofit organization devoted to research, education, and publication on important issues of domestic and foreign policy. Its principal purpose is to bring knowledge to bear on the major policy problems facing the American people.

On occasion Brookings authors produce research papers that warrant immediate circulation as contributions to the public debate on current issues of national importance. Because of the circumstances of their production, these Occasional Papers are not subjected to all of the formal review procedures established for the Institution's research publications, and they may be revised at a later date. As in all Brookings publications, the judgments, conclusions, and recommendations presented in the papers are solely those of the authors and should not be attributed to the trustees, officers, or other staff members of the Institution.

Contents

Preface

The United States and Russia stand at a critical threshold in their post–cold war relationship. The need to scale back and restructure the cold war defense industrial base is a challenge that both countries face. Although U.S. and Russian leaders recognize the value of making changes in this area, a variety of economic and political factors have slowed their realization, especially in Russia. In the meantime, both governments are pursuing expanded arms exports to support their struggling arms industries. Yet the two governments do not appear to recognize the long-term structural decline that is under way in international arms markets. As a consequence, neither will succeed in its export efforts. Worse, the resulting competition will likely produce increased security threats—in the form of technology and weapons proliferation, increased regional insecurity, and heightened political tension between the two countries.

Ironically, increased competition and its attendant risks run counter to fundamental—even revolutionary—changes that are occurring in the global security, technological, and economic environments. Coping with these new challenges will likely require a cooperative approach by the United States and Russia to the rationalization and conversion of their defense industrial sectors. In the near term, both states must adopt policies of restraint in arms sales while cooperating in their efforts to convert excess defense industrial capacities to civilian tasks. If implemented effectively, the Cooperative Threat Reduction Program, known as the Nunn-Lugar program, for assisting Russian defense conversion is an excellent step toward this end. In the longer term, both states should consider developing a new multilateral proliferation control regime and, perhaps, adopt a globalized approach to arms production.

This monograph is the product of the International Arms Sales Conference held by the Brookings Institution and the Institute for USA and Canada

Studies on February 3–5, 1994, in Queenstown, Maryland. Participants included representatives from United States and Russian defense industries as well as civilian analysts of security and defense industry matters. The aim of the conference was to explore the implications of the downturn in arms export markets and cooperative means for the United States and Russia to adjust to new defense industrial and security realities. The wide-ranging discussions provided a wealth of analyses, perspectives, and policy options. Although disagreements existed among the participants, they all shared the view that resolution of the problems related to arms export competition and defense industrial conversion will require a cooperative approach.

This monograph builds upon the conference discussions and papers, as well as additional research. Instead of producing an analysis and recommendations with which all the participants would agree, the organizers of the conference chose to enlist the rapporteur in drafting a report that synthesized the many spirited discussions. The resulting report, therefore, represents the views of the author alone.

The conference was generously supported by the Carnegie Corporation of New York. Conference participants on the American side were David Bernstein, Robert Cattoi, Jonathan Cohen, William Durch, Randall Forsberg, Clifford Gaddy, Jacques Gansler, Steven Irwin, Catherine Kelleher, Brett Lambert, Timothy McCarthy, Janne Nolan, Kevin O'Prey, James Roche, Andrew Solomon, John Steinbruner, and Charles Zraket. The Russian participants were Givi Dzhandzhgava, Aleksey Il'ichev, Valeriy Khrutskiy, Gennadiy Kotchetkov, Sergey Kulik, Mikhail Pogosyan, and Igor Stasevich.

Introduction

The end of the cold war presents the United States and the Russian Federation with dramatic new challenges. Because of fundamental shifts in the landscape of security relationships, armaments, and manufacturing technologies, major changes are needed in the approach that the two countries take in providing for their security. Continuing reliance on the cold war formula for security may pose increasing risks for the United States, Russia, and, ultimately, the rest of the globe. Most important, the immense defense industrial base of each country has become an economic burden as well as an impetus for weapons proliferation.

Instead of converting and fundamentally restructuring their respective cold war defense industries, the U.S. and Russian governments are attempting to shore them up, in large part by expanding arms exports. Unfortunately, this strategy poses a number of serious problems for both sides, not the least of which is that it simply will not succeed. The international demand for arms has declined precipitously in recent years. Even in the most optimistic of forecasts, arms exports cannot come close to compensating for the excess defense industrial capacity in both countries. Therefore, the need for rationalization and downsizing cannot be avoided. To the extent that the United States and Russia pursue arms export strategies in lieu of reforms, the two governments are wasting their limited resources on delaying hard choices that are probably inevitable. The consequences may be a renewed stockpiling of weapons, increased security risks, and the failure of Russian economic and political reforms.

Furthermore, regardless of the success or failure of arms export efforts, supplier competition poses serious long-term threats to the United States, Russia, and the rest of the world. Because international arms trade has become a buyer's market, the likelihood of proliferation of advanced, even state-of-the-art, weapon technologies has increased substantially. High-tech

3

arms proliferation can threaten U.S. and Russian interests by arming potential antagonists and by aggravating regional tensions generally. Increased export competition between Russia and the United States also poses a growing threat to their newly improved relationship. Both countries appear to have overly optimistic expectations of the potential returns from their arms export efforts. When these expectations are not fulfilled, the painful economic and social fallouts could engender bitterness between the two nations.

Collapse of demand for arms exports and excess defense industrial capacity are in part symptoms of ongoing revolutions in international security and industrial technology. Fundamental changes are occurring in the global security environment, as well as in the nature of armaments and manufacturing technologies. New strategies are required for building armed forces, managing defense industries, and stemming the proliferation of advanced technologies.

The United States and Russia stand at a major threshold in their relationship. In a number of obvious respects, their interests do not fully agree. Depending upon how the United States and Russia approach the changes that are afoot, either they may foster an environment of cooperative defense conversion or they may stumble back into renewed security competition. Strong incentives exist for the two states to adopt a cooperative approach to demilitarization, reduced arms exports, and security. To this end, a wide range of options are available for cooperative defense conversion, including policy measures that already are partly in place as well as much more radical joint institutional arrangements that can be considered in the future.

The Shrinking Global Arms Export Market

Throughout the cold war, the United States and the Union of Soviet Socialist Republics (USSR) were the only military powers that possessed defense industrial bases massive enough to provide for all of their armaments needs. The costs of maintaining these defense industrial bases were manageable largely because of the high levels of domestic arms procurement and the profound security concerns in both states. Although arms exports helped reduce production costs and served foreign policy ends, they were more of a luxury than a necessary component of defense policy.

As the United States, Russia, and other military powers have scaled back their defense orders for domestic consumption, the resulting overcapacity in their defense industries has made the need for alternative sources of procurement orders acute. Not surprisingly, exporting arms has become an attractive option. Unfortunately, at a time when they need help most, these countries must adjust to a new global environment in which opportunities to earn revenue abroad have diminished. The end of the cold war accelerated a trend of reduced global export demand for all types of armaments that has been under way since the mid-1980s (see figure 1).

In 1984 the size of the global arms export market was approximately $42.4 billion in constant 1990 dollars. Despite a brief surge caused by the intensification of the Iran-Iraq War, the demand for arms on the world market has been in sharp decline ever since. By 1993 the market had dropped to $21.9 billion, a little more than half its size a decade earlier. Although the decline may have reached its nadir, reasonable forecasts of future demand for arms indicate slight growth at most over the next decade. For example, one analysis predicted the level of arms export demand will be a relatively meager $15 billion in 1996, increasing to $18 billion by 2000.[1]

The decline in global demand for arms has affected the export success of all major players. Although the United States increased its share of the

Figure 1. Value of Global Exports: Major Conventional Weapons, 1984–93

Billions of 1990 U.S. dollars

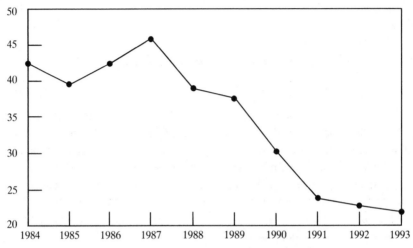

Source: *SIPRI Yearbook 1994* (Oxford University Press, 1994), appendix 13B, table 13B.2, p. 511; and *SIPRI Yearbook 1993: World Armaments and Disarmament* (Oxford University Press, 1993), pp. 476–77.

overall export total, the value of its major weapons exports declined by 42 percent in real terms from 1983 to 1992, according to the Institute for Defense and Disarmament Studies. USSR/Russia and France were hit even harder. During the same period, the value of the USSR/Russia's annual arms exports dropped by 86 percent; France, 72 percent. The United Kingdom, Germany, and the People's Republic of China experienced lesser, but still significant, declines.[2]

The lessening demand also has been reflected in production orders for U.S. and Russian arms manufacturers. For example, the Soviet Union between 1973 and 1982 produced on average 311 combat aircraft annually for export purposes. But in 1993 Russia may have produced as few as 79 aircraft for export. And an analysis of future demand indicates a decline to only 32 aircraft in 2000 (see figure 2). Similarly, the United States produced 256 combat aircraft for export per year on average during the 1973–82 period. In 1993, however, U.S. manufacturers may have produced only 71 aircraft for export. By 2000 the demand may be only 48 aircraft (see figure 3). Globally,

Figure 2. USSR/Russia Combat Aircraft: Production for Export, 1973–2000

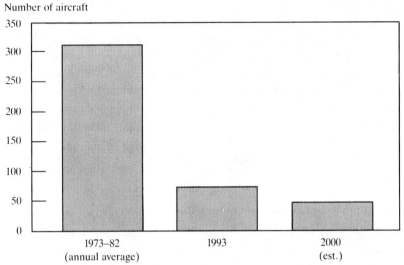

Source: Randall Forsberg, prepared for the International Arms Sales Conference, held by the Brookings Institution and the Institute for USA and Canada Studies, Queenstown Md., February 3–5, 1994.

Figure 3. U.S. Combat Aircraft: Production for Export, 1973–2000

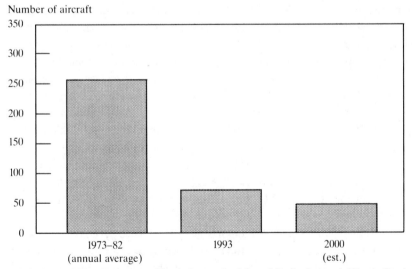

Source: Randall Forsberg, prepared for the International Arms Sales Conference, held by the Brookings Institution and the Institute for USA and Canada Studies, Queenstown Md., February 3–5, 1994.

on average more than 700 aircraft were produced annually from 1973 to 1982. But the 1993 level was only 222, and the expected global level in 2000 is 80.[3]

Although Russia was able to expand its arms export deliveries during 1993, these deals nonetheless represent a small fraction of those made in the early 1980s.[4] Moreover, the new export deals will not necessarily result in large hard currency revenues for the Moscow government or Russian defense enterprises. Some were in large part barter arrangements.[5] Other agreements to ship high-performance aircraft were swaps to cover Moscow's foreign debts.[6] For example, the Russian government settled some of its debts to Hungary with exports of MiG-29 aircraft. It sought to settle accounts with Germany and the Czech Republic similarly, but those efforts were unsuccessful.[7]

Reasons for the Decline

The decline in the global arms market resulted largely from the same factors that have reduced domestic demand for weapons in the United States and Russia. First and foremost is overcapacity brought on by the end of the cold war and by the defense buildups of the 1980s. The world is awash in excess weapons and defense production capacities. Most countries neither confront the threats to their security nor possess the economic means for maintaining their previous levels of militarization. Also, some formerly large importers such as India now prefer to develop and protect their own defense industries rather than buy abroad. In general, the countries that can afford to pay hard currency for weapons already possess more arms than they want, while those that desire foreign weapons do not have the money to buy them. As a result, prospective importers are more likely to upgrade their existing forces, not purchase expensive new systems. At a relatively low cost, upgrade programs can extend the life span and increase the combat capabilities of existing aircraft, combat vehicles, warships, and missiles.[8]

In addition, arms exporting states are confronting intensified competition on the supply side. Traditional arms exporters such as the North Atlantic Treaty Organization (NATO) states, Russia, China, Israel, and South Korea have been encountering new competition from developing producers such as India, Taiwan, and Brazil. Although high-performance systems—for example, combat aircraft—continue to be produced by only a few suppliers, new exporters have aggressively entered the market at the low and medium segments of the technological spectrum. For example, they now offer systems such as surface-to-surface missiles and tanks at competitive prices. These suppliers are also contributing to the increasingly competitive nature of the upgrades market.[9]

Furthermore, major military powers are willing to transfer huge quantities of redundant arms at bargain rates or for free. Arms control agreements, military force structure reductions, and continuing modernization programs have resulted in a glut of inexpensive older, but still effective, weapons that may compete directly against new systems in export markets. For example, the United States has given away equipment originally worth $2.5 billion to Greece, Turkey, Israel, Egypt, Morocco, Portugal, and Oman. Ironically, these efforts at times pit the uniformed military of a country—which wants to sell its redundant equipment—against its own industry.[10] U.S. industry officials estimated that fire sales of excess equipment could cost them up to $11 billion in foreign sales over the next several years, in addition to the $2.7 billion in foreign sales that they estimated as having already been lost.[11]

The severe decline on the demand side and overcapacity on the supply side of arms markets have created the worst case for both exporters and nonproliferation: a buyer's market. Because of the increasing competition between exporters, the profit margins for each sale are much smaller than in the past. Gone also are the days when the United States or Russia could sell their second-rate systems virtually off-the-shelf. Prospective arms importers have become much more demanding in terms of the top-of-the line equipment, coproduction agreements, offsets (requirements for local content and investment), countertrade requirements, and after-sale service.[12] As noted above, to cut deals, Russia has had to accept barter arrangements for their high-tech weapons.

Unfortunately, most American and Russian observers do not yet recognize the scale, long-term nature, and consequences of the global decline in arms exports. A 1993 survey found that U.S. defense industry executives were roughly evenly split between those who believed that foreign sales will increase and those who forecasted declining sales.[13] The problem is more pronounced in Russia, where the government and industry have engaged in costly wishful thinking. In 1992 the Ministry of Foreign Economic Relations anticipated export orders worth $3.1 billion and placed a comparable value of orders with defense enterprises. When actual deliveries reached only $1.1 billion, the ministry refused to pay the difference, and the defense enterprises were left holding their excess production.[14] Russian defense industry officials generally deny that the current low level of global demand for their arms is anything more than a temporary phenomenon caused by their government's incompetence, U.S. aggrandizement, or both. Many of them argue that with the proper government strategy Russia can increase its current real revenues from arms exports by more than ten times.[15]

The aims of Russian officials and industrialists who seek to reclaim the Soviet Union's past export success are quixotic. The decline in Russia in actual revenue is not as severe as it appears at first glance. Only a small proportion—approximately 25–33 percent—of Soviet arms exports historically were direct cash transactions. The bulk of Moscow's exports were for credit, much of which was never repaid. The reasons for this relate partly to Moscow's use of weapons transfers to serve its foreign policy goals.[16] As a consequence, the current revenue levels of Russian arms exports are not very different from the Soviet Union's actual hard currency earnings throughout the 1980s.[17] Achieving dramatic increases in revenues, therefore, may prove difficult.

Appeal of Arms Exports

How could the United States and Russia ignore the almost certain prospects for failure of export promotion strategies? The answer has much to do with the profound incentives for the defense industries and armed services of both countries to export weapons. The incentives for high levels of arms exports are always substantial. But these pressures become enormous when domestic demand for weapons procurement is in decline.

Incentives in the United States

One of the constant incentives is commercial: Arms exports can provide increased profit margins to producers. The greater the number of units that are procured at a price that exceeds the unit cost, the more the producer can amortize its overhead and development costs. In cases of mature systems— for example, the F-16—for which all the development costs have been covered, revenues in excess of unit costs are direct profits to the producer. Thus, when a system is coming to the end of its production life, a defense manufacturer has a great incentive to take advantage of existing tooling and workers to squeeze out a higher profit margin for the entire project.

Producers also seek arms sales to maintain efficient production rates— "smoothing out" production—as domestic demand declines. The natural cycles of development and production of weapon systems may require costly adjustments if a firm has to assemble large design and production teams with each new wave of work, only to let them go when the project slackens. By smoothing out their production rates with export orders, manufacturers hope to hang on to their development and production teams until work on the next generation system is ready to begin. For example, McDonnell-Douglas is attempting to maintain its F/A-18CD production with increased foreign orders. The firm then can hold its manufacturing base together until its next big project—the F/A-18EF—gets through the development process and is ready for production.

But the defense industries are hardly alone in pushing for exports. The armed services also have major budgetary incentives favoring exports. Because foreign sales help to reduce development and unit costs for the entire production run, the armed services benefit from the same kinds of economies of scale as industry when one of their systems is exported. They can obtain more weapons for the same amount of money. When a service is no longer procuring a particular system, foreign sales by industry help cover the development costs for the next generation system. For example, foreign sales of the F-16 help to absorb Lockheed Martin's overhead costs, thereby reducing the cost of F-22 development to the Air Force.

Incentives in Russia

Because of the excessive militarization of the Soviet economy, armaments are one of the few categories of Russian industrial products that are technologically competitive on the world market.[18] De facto subsidization of Russian defense output also encourages industry to export. Because many of their factor costs do not correspond to world levels, Russian defense enterprises can make substantial profits through arms exports.[19]

The Russian government, therefore, is actively encouraging its defense industry to export weapons. In so doing, it is seeking partly to reduce political pressure for subsidies to industry and partly to provide enterprises with financing for their conversion efforts.[20] Finally, the cash-strapped government can directly profit from arms sales through various fees and tariffs.

New Incentives for Both Countries

Numerous new factors are creating even more intense pressure for both countries to export weapons. The most important factor is the dramatic decline in domestic defense orders for virtually all defense producers. The collapse of domestic demand has sent most arms producers scrambling to find new markets; exports are a logical response. Also, governments might view export smoothing out as a cheap way to preserve their defense industrial bases. Furthermore, defense industry unemployment in regions such as California or Udmurtiya could pose serious political problems to any government in power.[21] And in Russia, the social and political consequences of defense industry unemployment could threaten the larger processes of political and economic reform.

Finally, even a goal of defense industrial conversion can provide big incentives for the export of weapons. States that are aiming to convert their excess defense industrial capacities to the civilian economy require huge amounts of investment and time. Given the global scarcity of government assistance and private investment for conversion, many defense firms and some governments view arms exports as a source of finance for their conversion efforts as well as a means to buy time for their industries to adjust.

The Trouble with Arms Exports

Whatever the short-term benefits of foreign arms sales, the effects of arms export competition are likely to threaten U.S. interests as well as aggravate global tension generally. Supplier competition alone will be very destructive, regardless of the success of various countries in their export efforts. Moreover, even the most plausible success in arms exporting would not enable the United States or Russia to absorb the overcapacity in their respective defense sectors. To the extent that the two governments pursue arms exports in lieu of defense industry restructuring and downsizing, they are merely putting off—and perhaps making more costly—inevitable hard choices.

U.S. Interests

Increased global arms export competition probably will have a negative effect on the four central threats to U.S. interests highlighted in the Bottom-Up Review conducted by the Department of Defense in 1993: weapons technologies proliferation, regional conflicts, undermining the preservation and protection of democracy, and economic security problems.

Arms exports contribute directly to the proliferation of weapons technologies. In a buyer's market and with intense competition among producer states, the likelihood that technologically state-of-the-art systems will be transferred on a wider scale is considerably greater. For example, to maximize its arms export potential, the Russian government is willing to sell some of its new high-tech weapons even before they are introduced into the Russian armed forces.[22] The growing use of coproduction agreements and licensing arrangements for foreign production of weapons also poses greater proliferation risks as production processes and technologies increasingly are transferred with the actual weapons.[23] Such technological diffusion will boost the military capabilities of states around the globe. The net effect could be that the United States, Russia, and other Western powers will feel compelled to increase the size and sophistication of their military forces.

In a competitive arms export environment, efforts to restrain sales to outlaw states or regional troublemakers are more difficult. If economic gain is the predominating motivation for competing suppliers, some state probably will transfer weapons to another's potential enemies. For example, although the United States views arms exports to Iran and Libya as threats to its interests, under conditions of unrestrained competition, other states, having failed in other markets, will be happy to fill Iranian and Libyan demand.[24]

Arms transfers are often directed to states that are involved in regional competition. As a consequence, they often contribute to spirals of increased regional insecurity and arms races. For example, new acquisitions by China are viewed with suspicion by East Asian countries, while exports to India cause concern in Pakistan. Increased regional instability—both in number of cases and their intensity—translates into greater problems for U.S. security planners and requires more U.S. forces to cope with them. One area of potentially serious concern is the Commonwealth of Independent States. Russia has identified the other former Soviet republics that make up the Commonwealth as an attractive target for its arms export efforts.[25] Given the political instability of some of those states and the numerous border disputes, further militarization of the region would be a troublesome development.

Arms exports also can have a negative impact on the goals of preserving and protecting democracies. Fostering new democracies probably requires a secure international environment. States that feel threatened may be less likely to undergo the difficult and often internally divisive process of democratization. In perhaps the most important case, to the extent that a faith in arms exports encourages the Russian government to delay measures of rationalization and downsizing of its defense sector, the success of Russian democratization and marketization efforts could be threatened. Continued subsidizing of the sizable Russian defense sector will certainly divert precious resources from more productive uses elsewhere in the economy. If the economic reform efforts were to fail, how the process of democratization could succeed is difficult to conceive.

Excessive competition over the shrinking arms export market will likely have a souring effect on relations among the competing supplier states. Although the absolute level of future exports for all suppliers will be much lower than it was in the early 1980s, some countries are suffering disproportionate losses. In particular, the United States will dominate the reduced export market while Russia will command a relatively smaller share.[26] The effect on the larger U.S.-Russian relationship will be negative. Russian industry representatives already argue that their failure to earn a living with exports is the result of the U.S. government's efforts to block them out of markets. Others argue against increased cooperation with NATO for fear that the West will impose standardization of weapons on eastern Europe and Russia, resulting in less demand for Russian arms.[27] However misguided these views may be, such misperceptions could foul the larger U.S.-Russian relationship.[28] All supplier states therefore must weigh the long-term consequences of a unilateral approach to the arms market.

Coping with Overcapacity

Arms exports ultimately may also harm U.S. and Russian economic security. In virtually every export forecast, both defense industrial bases will have immense overcapacity. The final report of the U.S. Defense Conversion Commission estimated that U.S. arms exports would have to double or triple to offset projected cutbacks in defense spending.[29] For example, the U.S. aviation industry produced on average almost six hundred combat aircraft per year between 1973 and 1982. However, firm or reliable orders have been placed for seventy-two aircraft in 2000.[30] Such small demand cannot support the five American manufacturers that produced fighter aircraft in 1982.

The situation for Russia is perhaps far more severe. The Russian Ministry of Defense has undertaken immense reductions in its procurement. Between 1991 and 1993 the Russian defense industries experienced a 78 percent drop in defense production.[31] The Russian Air Force is planning to reduce its number of aircraft by a third in 1994 alone.[32] Overall the Russian aerospace industry manufactured more than eight hundred combat aircraft on average annually during the 1973–82 period. But one estimate projected firm or reliable orders for only fifty-two aircraft in 2000.[33] This contracting market cannot support the five Russian design bureaus and the tens of production facilities that formerly were devoted to combat aviation.

The western European defense sector also has enormous excess capacity. In a defense market roughly half the size of that of the United States, western Europe has five major missile manufacturers compared with three in America, five combat aircraft producers versus two in the United States, and four tank producers compared with just one in the United States.[34]

Therefore, to the extent that the prospect of future arms exports provides declining industries in any of these countries with a reason to hang on, foreign sales are preventing the necessary rationalization and conversion of defense industrial bases. Struggling to survive with less business, declining defense firms may act as a drag on the national budgets and economies by extracting subsidies or other support from the government.

The Security and Technological Environment

A common thread links the pressure for arms exports, the serious problems associated with them, and the reasons that some officials and observers have been slow to recognize the likely consequences. Two revolutions—a security revolution and an industrial-technological one—will necessitate radical changes in the approach to security taken by the United States and, ultimately, the rest of the world. In this new environment, the maintenance of immense, isolated defense industrial bases will probably be neither economically feasible nor technologically sound. Furthermore, military operations in all likelihood will require forces different from a large standing military laden with expensive weapon platforms such as aircraft carriers or bombers. The advanced industrial states also will encounter greater difficulty preventing the proliferation of dual-use technologies that increasingly constitute the state-of-the-art military force. As a consequence, the issue confronting the United States, Russia, and the other military powers is how to reshape their sizable military and defense industrial establishments to fit new security, technological, and economic realities.

Security Revolution

The end of the cold war and the disintegration of the Soviet Union finally produced a long-heralded shift in the international security environment. Instead of a world characterized by two massive competing blocs of forces, the major military powers largely are now democratic states that are integrated into a nonconfrontational arrangement of economic interdependence. Even where they are not economically integrated, the threat of confrontation between military powers has diminished considerably.

The major powers face new types of security challenges. Large-scale ground force operations on short notice will probably not be the focus of defense planning for most countries. The security threats that the United States and other military powers will encounter are more likely to be lower in intensity and stem from problems of technology proliferation or the political disintegration of states. These problems are related more to conditions such as endemic economic austerity in highly populated regions than traditional state-versus-state conflict.[35] Moreover, international cooperative responses—whether by standing or ad hoc coalitions—are likely to be the norm.

Because of the security revolution, the dramatic decline in demand for defense production in most countries will continue. A need also will arise for a substantially different type of force posture from that fielded by the United States and Russia during the cold war. In most cases, armed forces will be oriented less toward massive armored conflicts and more toward flexible deployments in coalitional warfare. U.S. force levels envisioned in the Bottom-Up Review could be difficult to sustain politically and economically. Despite the Clinton administration's 1994 decision to increase defense spending through 2001, the lack of obvious military threats to core American security interests as well as pressures to increase domestic spending—for example, on entitlements or health care reform—will likely put continued downward pressure on the defense budget in the medium to long term. The Russian problem is qualitatively and quantitatively different; maintaining the size and type of forces called for by current military plans will be financially impossible. Generally, with the exception of a few militaristic countries, the end of the cold war has resulted in a paradoxical situation in which the states that want weapons cannot afford them, and many of the states that can afford them are not interested.

Technological Revolution

The radical shift in the global security environment is paralleled by a technological revolution in the advanced-industrialized states. This revolution is affecting the nature of particular armaments, the manufacturing processes used to produce them, and the ways that industry is organized generally.

New opportunities in the technological realm are leading to a sea change in the nature of arms and warfare. The growing availability of high-performance sensors, information processing capabilities, and precision-guided munitions—the elements of the so-called reconnaissance strike complex that was effective in the Persian Gulf War—is fundamentally changing combat operations.[36] Instead of traditional attrition warfare, reconnaissance strike combat is based on the integration of complex systems of highly accurate smart weapons and information-processing capabilities. The result will be less reliance upon expensive, vulnerable weapon platforms.

The new military systems will benefit from dramatic changes on the production-manufacturing side of the defense industry equation. The cold war formula of a large defense sector that is isolated from civil-commercial industry may have outlived its usefulness. As the nature of armaments is changing and industrial development overall is becoming increasingly sophisticated, characterizing specific technologies as either defense or commercial is difficult. The U.S. industries are increasingly falling behind the commercial sector in critical areas such as the development of cutting-edge technologies.[37] The commercial sector is also much better at integrating new technologies into products and quickly delivering them to the market. And the commercial side has had a much better record in keeping its production costs down.[38]

The direct impact of the technological revolution is not very evident in Russia, however. In the wake of the disintegration of both the economic planning system and the coherent military industrial complex in that country, talk about an ongoing technological revolution characteristic of an advanced industrial economy would be misleading. Although Russian industry possesses state-of-the-art technologies at the levels of basic research and early development, obsolescent production capacities have always proved to be a bottleneck in transferring these assets to the level of product manufacturing. Thus, a country rich with world-class physicists in the recent past produced weapons with vacuum tubes instead of electronic circuitry and televisions that were prone to explode in consumers' living rooms.

Nonetheless, the Russians are well aware of the significance of the security and technological revolutions. Former chief of the general staff marshall Nikolay Ogarkov argued in the early 1980s that the nature of warfare and armaments technology was undergoing fundamental changes that would require a revolutionary new approach to defense industry. During Mikhail S. Gorbachev's tenure, officials frequently expressed concern that improvements in accuracy were making conventional weapons comparable in destructive force to "weapons of mass destruction." And these concerns persist. The current long-term defense procurement plan of the Russian Ministry of Defense stresses the necessity of improved command, control, communications, and intelligence systems at the combat level.[39]

Consequences for Defense Industry

The security and industrial-technological revolutions will require radical transformations to the manner in which the U.S. and Russian defense planning systems provide for their security. Although the particular circumstances in the two states differ, both will have to downsize and rationalize their defense sectors, as well as convert unneeded assets to civilian use. A new approach to the defense industrial base will need to be adopted that stresses integration of the defense and civil-commercial sectors.

Conversion Imperative

Given the systemic defense industry overcapacity in the United States and Russia, both countries must convert a large part of their defense sectors to civilian tasks. Although the need for defense conversion is clear, the task has proved difficult to carry out in historical practice. Empirical evidence indicates that diversification to relatively similar products within a commercial plant on average is successful only half of the time. In the defense sector, the record is much worse. Attempts by defense plants to initiate production of new products for civilian consumption have experienced a meager 20 percent success rate.[40]

Thus the notion of simply redirecting existing defense production lines to new tasks is too simplistic. Historical experience suggests that conversion should have a broader definition, including diversification of defense companies through acquisition of civil-commercial assets, transfers of ownership of shares, sale of property, and reallocation of the labor force and managers to employment outside the initial plant.[41]

A number of axioms have evolved for reorienting defense plants. Perhaps the most important is the development of a "total business capability," which, for a particular company, includes an understanding of the market for the goods that it has chosen to produce, a reasonable plan for how it will get these products into the market, and the capacity to provide support after sale.[42] Many U.S. defense companies have found competing in civil-commercial markets difficult because they have become accustomed to working for a single customer (the federal government) who specifies exact requirements and imposes a high degree of regulation. Perhaps as a result, new product choices and specifications are often characterized by "technology push"—when the producer takes a technology that it knows well and builds a product to fit it with little thought of the ultimate market—instead of "demand pull." Most conversion successes have been achieved by locating growth markets and satisfying them, not attempting to sell modified military products to commercial markets.[43]

Thus, in seeking out new markets, the defense manufacturer should take advantage of its core competence while transforming its corporate culture from being a defense firm to a civil-commercial producer. Defense managers would benefit from a new self-image. They ought to consider themselves not as defense producers, but more generally as integrators of highly complex systems. As a general rule, they should aim to design new products for cost and efficiency, as opposed to high performance and durability, which are the requirements for defense products. Also, the groups related to the defense firm—labor, management, community leaders, and government officials—should be committed to the same goal.

Previous experience also revealed that conversion success is more likely when the new civil product requires a technological level comparable to the previous defense work. Defense firms that attempted to produce items of lesser technological levels generally have experienced failure. A firm's existing engineering innovation, capital equipment, production labor forces, and skilled management are its principle assets. In most cases, conversion success will depend upon how well they are utilized.[44]

The simple shifting of existing defense production facilities to new civil tasks is neither realistic nor a particularly good policy guide. Successful conversion usually requires restructuring and downsizing of a plant, as well as new acquisitions. In converting their enterprises, defense managers generally have had to liquidate some parts of their plants and facilities. For example, to compete in civil markets, many defense firms have had to streamline their engineering and administrative staffs. Furthermore, acquiring new civil assets might be the most direct means to diversification. Technology transfer from military to civilian purposes occurs perhaps most effectively through people working together. As a consequence, integrating staff with commercial backgrounds and those with defense production experience has been a successful strategy.[45]

Defense managers and government officials must also recognize that conversion is a long-term process. As the United States and Russia have learned, "peace dividends" do not mature quickly. Given the host of problems that develop both for commercial firms starting new production and defense plants seeking to convert, defense managers must adjust their conversion plans to play out over a period of years instead of months.[46]

An Integrated Civil-Commercial and Defense Industrial Base

Given reduced procurement levels, the increasing gap between the commercial and defense sectors, and advances in flexible manufacturing techniques, substantial incentives exist for the United States and other major industrial powers to restructure their defense sectors according to a new model of integrated defense and civil-commercial production.[47] Under this approach, the walls separating defense and civil production could be dismantled. The defense industry would simply be part of the larger industrial base and the government would be just another customer—ordering different goods and services. Integrated plants might primarily produce commercial items along with a few advanced military research and development (R&D) programs and a limited amount of advanced defense equipment production.[48] For example, the electronics industry could produce units for military consumption on the same production lines as commercial output. Both types of output could utilize commercial components, software, materials, and manufacturing equipment. Also, artillery perhaps could be made on the same rotary forge as railroad freight car axles.[49]

Some defense plants will be needed, but in greatly reduced numbers. Furthermore, the uniqueness of defense-specific plants would be determined by their particular production processes, not by their output, which is directed toward military uses.[50] When civil and military output cannot be manufactured on the same production line, they ideally would be produced in a diversified company with the emphasis on sharing of technology between the civil-commercial and defense operations. Western European defense companies often already are dual-use technology firms, with their most profitable operations lying in the civil sector.[51]

The integrated approach would require substantial change in the way that the U.S. Department of Defense procures weapons. In particular, the federal government would need to abolish, among other things, its unique procurement practices, cost accounting methods, and military specifications and standards. Ideally, no unique laws or regulations requiring a separation of commercial and defense operations would apply to the purchase of defense goods and services.[52] The Clinton administration and the Defense Department under Secretary William J. Perry have already taken significant steps in this direction.

Options for U.S. Defense Industry

In adapting to new security, technological, and economic conditions, the U.S. government and industry can choose between three models or strategies for organizing the future defense industrial base.

The first, Status-Quo Minus, represents a continuation of the existing formula—an isolated, unique, defense industrial base—albeit at reduced scale. The government would use existing procurement and accounting practices. The barriers between defense producers and civil-commercial industry would probably persist. However, the number of defense producers would drop, largely through market consolidation, to correspond to lower demand for forces.

Under the second model, Dual-Use/Civil-Military Integration of Industry, the walls between defense and civil-commercial business would be broken down as much as possible. Instead of having separate defense producers, civil and defense production would occur on the same flexible manufacturing lines.

The third model is Multilateral Cooperative Production. Although the process of globalization and interdependence of defense industries is still a novelty, like-minded states within a few years may take advantage of an international division labor and manufacture their defense products jointly. No state would then possess a comprehensive defense industrial base capable of independently supplying all its defense procurement needs. Ultimately, this arrangement might even include former adversaries such as the United States and Russia. Because old habits and suspicions die hard, the third option is probably infeasible in the near term. But if the United States, Russia, and other major military powers manage their relations carefully, the approach could be adopted on a broad scale as early as the beginning of the twenty-first century. Several western European states already have taken steps in this direction.[53]

The first strategy ignores emerging security, technological, and economic realities. When the demand for new defense systems will be numbering in the tens instead of the hundreds, the preservation of a comprehensive, isolated defense industrial base is an extremely costly, if not unrealistic, proposition.[54] Given that the greatest advances in technology are occurring in civil-commercial development and manufacture, the United States would be restricting its development of military systems. Moreover, if a revolutionary change in armaments technologies and employments is occurring, scarce defense monies should not be wasted on preserving production facilities for yesterday's weapons technologies and armaments.

Therefore, the second option appears to be the most prudent course for the near term. It offers defense producers an opportunity to diversify while encouraging a more systematic interaction in technologies—"spin-offs" and "spin-ons"—between civil and defense manufacturing. It also offers the most flexibility for future adaptation to new manufacturing and technology demands.

What kinds of changes to the US defense industrial base would be necessary under the dual-use model? Firms that are almost exclusively involved in defense production—for example, Northrop-Grumman—would find their options limited. Only a small number of pure-defense producers are likely to survive.[55] Companies already well diversified into civil-commercial production have a much better chance, although they probably will have to convert further their defense producing capabilities to strictly civil production or according to the dual-use model.[56]

PURE-DEFENSE PRODUCERS. Pure-defense producers will separate into three distinct groups: those that consolidate themselves as more efficient defense producers, those that become de facto arsenals, and those that liquidate.

The first group of producers, which includes Lockheed Martin, Loral, and Northrop-Grumman, will pursue the strategy of consolidation in defense business through mergers, acquisitions, and a streamlining of assets. In this strategy, a firm's board of directors and shareholders are betting that by acquiring competitors' defense assets, or merging with them outright, the resulting firm will be one of the few survivors in the smaller defense market.[57]

The second group are the small number of firms that possess unique capabilities. With the support of the government, some parts of these defense companies could survive by transforming themselves into arsenals. General Dynamics appears to have adopted this strategy for the assets that it did not sell off.[58]

For those companies that cannot win in the defense merger and acquisition game and that cannot transform themselves into an arsenal, they must liquidate. Conversion or diversification is not an option because pure-defense firms confront serious barriers when attempting to take on civil-commercial pursuits. In general, stockholders do not trust pure-defense companies to make wise conversion choices. Stockholder reasoning goes: "If we wanted to be involved in civil-commercial stockholding, we would invest in a firm that specializes in that area." Ergo, the stockholders prefer liquidation. If a company's management attempts to convert, it faces the unpalatable prospect of shareholder revolt or desertion, leading to a depreciation in the firm's value. General Dynamics' management may have anticipated a similar scenario when it decided to sell off the aircraft business to Lockheed, the tactical missile business to Hughes, and the space work to Martin Marietta.

DIVERSIFIED PRODUCERS. U.S. defense producers that are already diversified into civil-commercial production will have a wider range of options when adapting to the new environment. As diversified firms, they do not face the same structural, regulatory, and shareholder barriers to conversion that confront exclusively defense firms. Diversified firms benefit from fewer information barriers when shifting defense technologies to civil pursuits because they have civil-commercial capabilities, figuratively speaking, under the same roof. In terms of government regulation, defense firms possessing commercial subsidiaries can more easily spin-off their defense technologies or processes.[59] Furthermore, shareholders of diversified firms are more likely to trust the decisions of their corporate board to convert further their defense assets. Conversion or increased diversification of the firm's portfolio appears to be the strategy used by Rockwell and Raytheon.[60]

Thus, already diversified firms are the ideal candidates to create and employ dual-use production facilities. The only other alternative is complete conversion: getting totally out of defense. For example, General Electric, a previously diversified firm, sold off all of its defense assets to focus on its core commercial business.

Environment for Russian Industry

Although defense industry problems are generally the same in Russia and the United States, Russia in many ways confronts more difficult obstacles with much more serious consequences. While the federation government has been transforming the formerly command system to a free-market economy, Russia has been undergoing a historically unprecedented conversion of thousands of enterprises.[61] The Russian defense industry confronts four challenges, each of which alone might seem insurmountable: (1) Russian defense procurement for most weapons has declined to relatively negligible levels; (2) the poor performance of the economy has led to a dearth of state and private investment in the defense sector; (3) the transformation of the economy has created a highly unstable business environment; and (4) most defense enterprises must undertake fundamental restructuring.

The demilitarization of the Russian economy is a Herculean task. The entire Soviet command economy was organized to support defense production. The defense industries accounted for approximately 60 percent of machine production and more than 80 percent of electronics manufacturing in the Soviet economy. The defense industries also had priority access to the best resources and labor in the Soviet system; the civil economy was left with the residual.

Not only have Russian defense enterprises been cut off from most of their former perquisites, but they have also experienced cuts in weapons procurement on a much greater scale than those in the United States. Overall, Russian defense procurement has been reduced by 83 percent from 1990 to 1993.[62] Arms that in the past were procured at rates of several hundred or more annually now are being procured in tens or less.[63]

The disastrous state of the Russian economy has made obtaining investments extremely difficult for defense enterprises even for their daily operations, much less their long-term programs or conversion. As a consequence, many have shortened their workweeks, sent their employees home on unpaid leaves, or delayed paying salaries for as long as three months.[64]

The economic crisis has starved the government of resources required to meet the most rudimentary defense procurement and conversion plans. The Ministry of Defense of the Russian Federation, for example, is attempting to scale back its armed forces and the defense industrial base. Planned procurement levels are based on an armed forces structure that will be less than half the size of the Soviet military in the mid-1980s.[65] Yet even after these reductions, the ministry probably will not be able to afford its force structure. An analysis of comparative Russian force levels and their financial requirements found that the cost for the force structure proposed by the Ministry of Defense for 1995—a 1.5 million-person force—could exceed the 1994 defense budget by a factor of three.[66] Similarly, government officials responsible for the defense industries argued that conversion would cost 554 billion rubles.[67] Although the reliability of these estimates is questionable, they dwarf the less than 50 billion rubles that the Russian government has been spending annually in support of conversion.

Russian defense enterprises also must cope with the transformation from a command system to a market economy. Basic market mechanisms that firms need to survive are lacking. For example, stable rules of the game for free-market activity have not yet developed sufficiently. As a result, new supplier or purchaser relationships between enterprises are not easy to establish. Poorly developed labor and housing markets make it harder for managers to release redundant labor—because employees have no place to go—and to hire new workers and specialists. Weak capital markets and the rudimentary nature of the private banking system make obtaining investment capital very difficult.

In addition, Russian defense enterprises themselves must undergo fundamental restructuring. Organized to operate in a command economy, the Russian defense industry is poorly suited to the demands of market competition. Many large enterprises are burdened with costly social support obligations for their workers—providing apartments, kindergartens, health facilities, and so on—that would be the responsibility of local government in other countries. Russian defense enterprises also tend to be autarkical in their organization. Because of the vertical integration and the chronic shortages in the Soviet economy, defense managers sought to reduce uncertainties by producing as much of their required supplies in-house as possible. As a result, Russian enterprises often are oversized organizations that ignore the value of a division of labor with other firms.[68]

Similarly, the corporate culture of a Russian defense enterprise resembles an arsenal more than a free market or monopsony. Although most defense companies are privatizing, they have little practical experience operating independently of the state.[69] This problem exists for defense firms in the West as well, but it is much more pronounced in Russia. Russian firms are in need of a total business capability, which includes operations that are taken for granted in any free-market company: market research, designing products for cost efficiency, and marketing goods effectively. Russian defense enterprises traditionally have been oriented toward a "supply-push" approach to developing and manufacturing new products; because consumers were undemanding or had no influence, the quality and specifications of products were determined independent of them. Most Russian firms must completely reorient themselves toward a demand-pull approach, in which product costs, specifications, and design are determined by market demand.[70]

Finally, in contrast to the situation in the United States and elsewhere, the Russian government and industry risk social instability in their efforts to rationalize the defense industrial base. The combined problems of an economy in depression, a slowly developing labor market, and the dependence

trust, cooperative efforts will have to be based on direct and immediate complementarity of interests, such as jointly redirecting military technologies to commercial purposes.

Ultimately, control of armaments proliferation and dual-use technologies will probably require a new multilateral institution aimed at creating greater transparency in international trade. To provide participants with adequate incentives to adhere to the rules, any restraint and transparency regime must include a set of political and economic benefits that form a foundation on which to build a larger security partnership between the United States and Russia. Such a partnership could and, perhaps, should eventually lead to joint U.S.-Russian production of armaments.

A number of mechanisms already are in place that can be adapted or enlarged for the task of cooperation. Most important, in recent years countries in the industrialized world have demonstrated a willingness to exert leadership in fostering military restraints, including lending assistance to states interested in arms reduction or nonproliferation regimes. The most prominent example is the expanding financial and technical assistance provided to the former Soviet states for the purpose of disarmament.[71] Some of the most promising efforts are oriented toward developing Russian enterprises into viable businesses at the ground level with the help of U.S. partners.

Successful cooperation in defense conversion and limiting proliferation ultimately will require involvement by the governments and business communities in both countries. Any efforts must respect the comparative advantages of government policy and private enterprise activity, enlisting each to do what it does most effectively. While the respective governments must provide the impetus and context for cooperation, ventures by private enterprise should shoulder most of the burden—and economic benefits—of the cooperative process.

Nonthreatening Security Environment and Export Restraint

The first prerequisite to U.S.-Russian cooperation in arms exports and adjustment of defense industries is a stable, nonthreatening, international security environment. Neither government is likely to feel secure enough to carry out a substantial conversion of its defense industrial base if it fears that its former adversary is not behaving similarly. Regardless of real intentions, most cooperation—whether bilateral or multilateral in scope—depends upon universality of sacrifice. In Russia, for example, the domestic political climate has turned hostile toward perceived unilateral security concessions to the West. And in the United States, despite the virtual disappearance of the USSR/Russian threat, substantial domestic resistance still exists to reductions in the armed forces and the defense industrial base from their cold war levels. Economic forces probably will continue to drive Russian defense allocations to lower levels, and the United States should maintain a degree of symmetry in force reductions and conversion of defense industry. Otherwise, a souring of relations between the two states may result.

Both the United States and Russia should also reverse their current policies and restrain their arms export efforts. Both governments are encouraging and assisting their arms industries to export. To avoid the dangers of excessive export competition, both should divorce themselves from pursuing arms exports for economic gain or in lieu of a practical defense industrial base strategy. As the United States controls more than half of the supply-side of the global arms export market, it bears the greater responsibility. Its commitment to restraint will have an immediate, profound impact. For its part, Russia should institute a credible export control regime that reaches the enterprise level.[72] Moreover, if the two governments cooperate, they can then use their combined influence to press other defense producers to restrain their efforts.

Although attempting to ban arms sales outright would be fruitless, in the spirit of restraint, the major exporters should impose certain criteria upon themselves. For example, some enterprises could be permitted to export their armaments if they demonstrate that they have a credible plan for taking the proceeds and using them to fund conversion. Approval for arms transfers for the enterprises should be tied to a specific period of time after which a review could be undertaken to verify that they are not squandering their export revenues. The overriding goal would be to assist reform-oriented defense enterprises to convert, not to give breathing room to enterprises with conservative approaches.

Although some level of arms exports will continue to be necessary for virtually all defense producing states, each would benefit from the establishment of broader institutional measures for increased transparency and confidence-building. One of the main benefits would be to verify that one country is not attempting to take advantage of the restraint of others. Measures could include prior notification of transfers of major weapon systems to keep aggregate sales consistent with reasonable levels of global deployment.[73] Even more effective would be an arrangement among the major exporters to create an exhaustive registry to enable accurate monitoring of market transactions for all potentially dual-use systems and technologies. This would be a central element of a multilateral cooperative security system.

Rationalization of Defense Sectors

Self-imposed restraint, unfortunately, will not do the job on its own. Both the United States and Russia should take steps to reduce the sources of domestic political pressure for arms exports and high levels of defense spending. Perhaps the only means to this end is the prompt rationalization of defense industrial bases. Instead of continuing with an ad hoc approach, both governments would ultimately benefit by making difficult, but necessary, choices between winners and losers in their respective defense industrial bases. Ideally, the governments would move quickly to identify the companies or enterprises—or, at the very least, the capabilities—that are critical defense industrial assets and provide them with adequate business or state support.[74] The remaining, nonessential enterprises should be cut off from state funding and told to either convert to civil-commercial pursuits or shut down. The two governments would be allocating their limited defense resources most efficiently and sending clear signals to enterprises that must convert or liquidate. Moreover, by cutting off the losers, each state can more effectively use revenues—whether from the state budget or from limited arms exports—on the arms producers that remain.

Rationalization is a step that each country would have to take on independently. Although the other state can help in providing a stable, non-threatening security environment, each state is essentially alone in making the hard choices. Neither government will be willing to allow the other, at least initially, to have a role in defense industrial decisions that it deems to be tightly tied to its national security.

Cooperation in Conversion

The area in which coordinated efforts between the United States and Russia will play a key role will be in aiding the transition for those enterprises that are not the priorities of the respective ministries of defense. A vital need exists for cooperation in finding new work for nonessential enterprises. Each country would benefit from the dismantling of the industrial basis for the threat to one another. Industries in both countries would gain economically from cooperation. For Russian enterprises undergoing conversion, cooperation might be the only way to obtain the necessary financing and market training. Collaboration with U.S. high-tech or other commercial firms could help them develop the total business capability that will be necessary for their survival in a free market.

American firms would benefit from access to Russian technologies, such as optics and lasers, or to new markets through Russian joint ventures.[75] Because the Soviet defense sector had concentrated within it, by and large, the best technologies and human capital, its remnants are the obvious candidates for Western cooperation. Despite the many obstacles, real opportunities are available for Western business in Russia, according to U.S. firms that are involved in joint ventures with Russian enterprises. For example, the Lockheed Corporation experienced impressive success in its joint space launch venture with two Russian partners. Before Lockheed's merger with Martin Marietta, the joint project had lined up $600 million in contracts to launch communications satellites.[76] This success is likely to expand for the new Lockheed Martin corporation.

Industry perhaps is at an advantage and governments at a disadvantage in conversion cooperation. The Russian and U.S. defense sectors do not necessarily require a massive aid program. Channeling large sums of money into either country's defense industries will hardly provide incentives to change. Instead, the key may be to put the defense sectors to work on productive tasks that can sustain themselves financially. Ultimately, successful business cooperation would provide far more resources to the Russian economy than any aid program could ever hope.[77] Although governments can and should provide an environment in which joint contacts can flourish, bureaucrats in general do not excel at locating creative business opportunities or distributing resources in an optimal way. Moreover, private enterprise generally fare better when not bound by the restrictions that accompany government programs. Entrepreneurs can assess risks and sound investments and adopt flexible strategies to cope with them in ways that governments are not positioned to do. Thus, to the extent possible, government should help lay the basis for business cooperation and then step out of the way.

In creating the conditions for free enterprise and cooperation between U.S. and Russian business to flourish, the Russian government should adopt a number of vital measures. Western businesses rightly complain about a wide range of obstacles to successful business ventures in Russia. The Russian government should establish more effective formal rules, regulations, and procedures for its economy. Without them, the restructuring of the economy and the opportunities for foreign investment will be limited. For example, the government would be wise to increase the pace of, and limit the restrictions on, privatization in the defense sector. By allowing a defense plant to privatize, the government permits it the legal autonomy that would make it a more attractive prospect to Western investors.[78] The federation government should also create a more solid legal basis for small enterprise spin-offs from larger enterprises.[79] Ideally, the Russian government ultimately will permit foreign ownership of the small enterprises.[80]

The Russian government should immediately adopt two other measures with the aim of fostering foreign direct investment. First, the government must develop a legal basis for intellectual property rights. Currently, Western businesses must fend for themselves by developing situation-specific arrangements with their Russian counterparts to protect their intellectual property rights. This time-consuming and uncertain process likely deters some Western businesses from seeking out Russian partners and raises the costs for those that do get involved. Second, the Russian government should rewrite its regulations to help Western businesses repatriate their profits directly. Current regulations, adopted for short-term benefit, are inhibiting the flow of private investment because many Western firms are having too much trouble getting their earnings out of Russia in valuable form.

Actions required of the U.S. government to encourage industry cooperation are qualitatively different. To foster a lasting, valuable US-Russian partnership, the U.S. government should encourage U.S. industry to take the lead. But industry will require some government backing to help overcome the initial obstacles and uncertainties of foreign investment. Thus, the U.S. government need not fund U.S. businesses with government contracts. Instead, it should be providing security and financial backing to help companies reduce the risks of pursuing their own profit-seeking activities. The formula for any aid should be that the ultimate revenues must come from joint private sector business activity, not government contract work.

A wide range of options are available to the U.S. government, and fortunately, most cost relatively little and promise enormous returns. The Overseas Private Investment Corporation (OPIC) provides direct loans to small and medium-size companies for investment insurance in developing countries to hedge against a variety of political risks.[81] The Clinton administration has also used the Agency for International Development's Enterprise Fund to finance joint ventures.

While these programs have been very successful, the scale and unique character of cooperative defense conversion require a different instrument.

Perhaps the best candidates are an expansion of the Cooperative Threat Reduction Program—known as the Nunn-Lugar program for its congressional sponsors, Sens. Sam Nunn, D-Ga., and Richard G. Lugar, R-Ind.—developed to assist the denuclearization of the former Soviet states or the adoption of a National Academy of Sciences proposal called a Russian-American Partnership for Industrial Development (RAPID).[82]

The Nunn-Lugar Program

The Nunn-Lugar program originally was conceived as a means of helping the states of the former Soviet Union dismantle their nuclear weapons and for stemming the dangers of proliferation of weapons of mass destruction.[83] Since fiscal year 1993 the scope of the Nunn-Lugar program has been expanded to include funds for the conversion to civilian purposes of defense industries in the post–Soviet states.[84] The fiscal 1994 authorization provided for four distinct programs: (1) "The Fast Four"; (2) direct aid for joint ventures of U.S. firms with an additional eighty-two enterprises; (3) the Prefabricated Housing Initiative; and (4) the Demilitarization Enterprise Fund (or the Defense Enterprise Fund).

The Fast Four are pilot projects involving Russian defense enterprises that have been targeted for a streamlined process of creating joint ventures with U.S. firms.[85] Approximately $20 million has been awarded to four projects that pair U.S. firms with the enterprises to create a new venture oriented toward production of goods and services for the Russian civil economy, including dental chairs, cola processing and bottling, hearing aids, and new air traffic control systems.[86] The U.S. government is providing "seed capital" to which the business partners must add contributions of financing, capital, labor, and so on.[87]

In addition to the Fast Four, the Department of Defense plans to fund eighty-two more enterprises according to the same model, but in a less expedited manner. The U.S. Defense Nuclear Agency will provide awards valued at $1 million to $5 million for projects with these companies. The U.S. government would contribute only seed capital with the aim of fostering a long-term business partnership between the American and Russian partners.

The Prefabricated Housing Initiative includes $20 million for joint U.S.-Russian production of prefabricated housing for demobilizing Russian officers. Five Russian enterprises have been selected as candidates to pair with U.S. firms and convert part of their facilities to the production of prefabricated housing.[88] The program aims to capitalize these enterprises so they have a high probability of succeeding in the ruble economy.

The Demilitarization Enterprise Fund will be the primary means of U.S. assistance to the conversion of Russian enterprises. The fund is a nonprofit organization established to provide financial support to joint business initiatives for defense conversion in Russia, Belarus, and Ukraine. Although the fund will be capitalized by the Department of Defense, its operations will be completely independent of the government. Its efforts will concentrate on joint initiatives between U.S. firms and privatizing defense enterprises. The fund will focus in particular on firms that were formerly involved in the production of weapons of mass destruction. Its mechanisms for providing support include making equity investments, offering loans or grants, and providing collateral for loans.[89]

Overall the four defense conversion programs are an innovative and extremely promising expansion of the Nunn-Lugar process. Each of the programs has the virtue of stressing business partnerships that will be both profitable and enduring. Ideally, the U.S. government will provide only limited resources at the outset to get the project off the ground. The emphasis on enterprises that are privatizing encourages both the conversion and the restructuring of the Russian defense sector. The partnership aspect of the program should foster the transmission of business and market skills between American and Russian firms. Joint programs should also facilitate the transfer of valuable technologies between the two countries.

The Prefabricated Housing Initiative represents an outstanding example of cooperative work that is in the mutual interests of the United States and Russia. The Russian military is able to reduce its numbers with less fear of social tensions because retiring soldiers have a place to live. Russian enterprises benefit because they have profitable tasks—building the prefab units—to which to convert, and the U.S. prefabricated housing industry benefits by finding new partners, new markets, and new state-backed work.

The primary drawback of the conversion programs has been the funding mechanism. Until fiscal year 1994 spending for the Cooperative Threat Reduction Program was authorized by the U.S. Congress, but the program was not provided with its own earmarked appropriation. Instead, funding was transferred from the Department of Defense budget, a process that proved cumbersome.[90] Because of the indirect funding procedure and the bureaucratic obstacles found in Russia, actual spending of the money has been slow. Out of $1.2 billion authorized by Congress for Nunn-Lugar programs during the fiscal years 1992–94, only $223 million had been spent as of June 1994. The delay proved costly as authority for $212 million expired, which meant the funding could not be spent.

The effectiveness of the Nunn-Lugar program would be vastly improved through a refinement of the funding mechanism. Fortunately, Congress has begun earmarking funds for the Cooperative Threat Reduction Program as a line-item within the defense budget. Whether this step will alleviate the problem of delays in the process of funding specific projects remains to be seen.

The Clinton administration and Congress should also devote more resources to strictly enterprise conversion activities. Although the initial denuclearization focus of the Nunn-Lugar program continues to be extremely important to demilitarize the Russian economy over the long term. The emphasis should perhaps shift to enterprise conversion and restructuring. Furthermore, conversion and partnership efforts should be directed toward all defense enterprises, not just those associated with weapons of mass destruction.

Some aspects of how the Demilitarization Enterprise Fund will work are not clear. In particular, whether the fund will be capitalized adequately by the U.S. Congress is uncertain. If funding proves to be inadequate, a potential modification would be to restructure the fund into a profit-making venture sustained by private investment.

RAPID

An alternative initiative that would stress private investment and could result in profits for the U.S. government is the cooperative defense conversion proposal advanced by a 1993 National Academy of Sciences study. RAPID would encourage U.S. and Russian economic cooperation at the level of private enterprise and create incentives for the establishment of new free market-oriented firms in the Russian economy. The goal is to create cooperative business ventures that are profitable in and of themselves and are thus sustainable, as in the Nunn-Lugar program.

The U.S. and Russian governments would set up the initial RAPID program and a highly visible, joint Russian-American agency with its own governing board and management. The RAPID board would select specific joint-investment projects proposed by individual American and Russian enterprises. These projects would involve the purchase of capital goods and related services from the U.S. partner for use on Russian soil to produce civilian goods primarily for the domestic Russian market.[91]

Payment for the American goods and services would be in ruble-denominated shares in newly created Russian enterprises that are organized to acquire goods and services. The new Russian enterprises would be jointly owned by the Russian enterprise that sponsors the project, the American supplier, and the RAPID fund. The shares financed through RAPID would be pooled into an investment fund, in which dollar-denominated securities would be sold through underwriters to private investors. The U.S. partner would be required to retain some equity position—perhaps 10 percent—of these new Russian shares. The balance of the Russian shares issued to the American supplier would be financed through RAPID.

The RAPID program would require some initial assistance from the U.S. and Russian governments. For example, the U.S. government might guarantee a bridge loan for up to two years from the start of the program to get a number of projects up and running before RAPID approaches the capital markets to raise equity funds.[92] After the start-up phase, RAPID would raise capital for projects by issuing fund shares in Vintage series. For the investment fund to be marketable, both governments would need to provide a joint and several guaranty for the full dollar amount of the original investment after five years from issuance, regardless of the shareholder.[93] However, as compensation for the guaranty, the Russian and U.S. governments would each be entitled to 5 percent of the profits of the investment fund. Because RAPID relies on the capital markets to provide funding for its projects and utilizes a five-year guaranty, the costs of the program during the first six or seven years (up to two years for the bridge loan and five years for the guaranty on the first series of RAPID shares) would be modest. Furthermore, if RAPID were not successful, the costs of fulfilling the guaranty would not have a significant impact on the budgets of the U.S. and Russian governments until six or seven years from the program's inception, and these cash costs, if any, would be spread out over several years because of the issuance of RAPID shares in Vintage series (see appendix).[94]

Direct Assistance

Although industry-industry partnership should be the centerpiece of immediate U.S.-Russian efforts at cooperation, a number of areas exist in which direct assistance by the United States to Russian projects would be extremely valuable to Russian defense conversion, marketization, and democratization, as well as U.S. employment. One key area would be technical assistance to regional and local governments. Under the Soviet system, these institutions had a small role in governing and providing services for the local population. For example, many Russians obtained their apartments and social support through their place of employment. But today local governments must assume the new role of provider and representative for their local populations. They could use Western technical assistance in determining how best to provide services and what their most effective role would be. They would also benefit from assistance in such basic areas as financing and budgeting, tax systems, and fostering local industry and commerce. The risk of social instability makes the need for assistance in defense regions particularly acute.

Another area in which direct assistance is worth expanding relates to resolving the problems of the limited housing market in Russia. One of the main barriers to the necessary closing of enterprises on a wide scale across Russia is the restricted mobility of the labor force as a result of the chronic shortage of housing. Until the housing crisis is alleviated, the development of a flexible labor market will be hindered. Under the Nunn-Lugar program, the U.S. government is financing the creation of housing for retiring Russian soldiers. The United States and the West should consider expanding the process to help Russian enterprises produce more private housing across all of Russia.

Russia also requires direct technical assistance in developing its own export control system. The director of export controls for the Ministry of Foreign Affairs argued that Russia requires expertise from the West to organize export controls at the level of private enterprises and industries.[95]

Finally, the obsolescent and underdeveloped infrastructure in Russia provides an uncertain foundation on which to build a new market economy. Virtually all of Russia's economic infrastructure—from telecommunications networks to air traffic control systems, airports, and highways—requires large-scale development. U.S. industry is well suited to carrying out infrastructure development, particularly if it enlists Russian partners. For example, U.S. and Russian aerospace companies could design and implement new air traffic control systems for the Russian Far East and Siberia. Such an effort could be financed partially through international aid and partly, perhaps, by payments in Russian natural resources.[96]

Future Collaboration

The United States and Russia should consider future arrangements in which security and economic cooperation are more firmly institutionalized.

Although many proposed measures seem idealistic, they would be wholly realizable and mutually beneficial if the logic of cooperation and mutual interest is pursued to its obvious conclusion. The measures represent the culmination of current trends toward global integration and a multilateral approach to the provision of security.

Multilateral Proliferation Control

The long-term solution to the arms and technology proliferation problem will probably depend on the creation of a multilateral regime based on transparency and restraint in trade. The increasingly dual-use nature of high technology and the increased interdependence of the global economy make the prospects poor for any multilateral arms export regime based on denial. Past efforts to limit armaments transfer illustrate that restraints that depend solely on supplier cartels are doomed to failure. Policies that appear to be discriminatory are similarly unsuccessful. Furthermore, a comprehensive control effort could do more harm than good. Even if it failed as a control mechanism, such an institution might nonetheless inadvertently obstruct the flow of international trade. Thus, control agreements must ultimately focus on the demand side and at least aspire to universality.[97]

To allow for the continued integration and liberalization of the world economy as well as effective control, a new approach is necessary. Instead of export control based on licensing a wide range of dual-use technology transfers, an international registry and a regulating regime providing full disclosure of the intended application of the technology would be more effective and would reduce the burden of regulation.[98] The essence of such a system would be transparency: Although trading arrangements would be more open, they would be subject to requirements for disclosure of technology applications in a system that monitors and records trade flows internationally.[99] Because of the difficulty of monitoring increasingly complex networks of producers and dual-use technologies, regulators would impose their information-gathering efforts at a different stage in the life cycle of the product— further upstream in the chain of proliferation, closer to or at the level of production.[100]

The basis for the regime would be the establishment of an institution that requires the registration and monitoring of all companies involved in the production or transfer of sensitive dual-use goods and technology; for example, an Automated Technology Transfer Registry (ATTR). Any transparency or registry system would monitor transactions of potentially dual-use technologies both within a single country and abroad. A specially designed computer program would trigger a warning if a planned transfer did not comply with the parameters set by the program. Among other criteria, these parameters would stipulate that (1) transfers take place only among companies that are registered with the ATTR; (2) transfers take place only if all the required information—including destination, recipient, and purpose of end use—is furnished; (3) transfers be checked against a proscribed product and destination list that includes countries and end users and is regularly updated; and (4) transfers be checked for possible piecemealing by the same supplier or across several suppliers.[101]

Although a regulating regime may seem cumbersome, it would ultimately represent a dramatic improvement over current arrangements in effectiveness and relieving the burden on regulated actors. If the regulations replace the needless intrusions on legitimate trade that are at the core of grievances about existing regimes and still protect credible nonproliferation objectives, they would likely be welcomed by the participants.[102] Moreover, transparency and regulatory regimes function well and relatively burden-free in a variety of markets.

Although a regulatory arrangement ideally would have universal membership, in its founding it could be comprised of only a few key members.[103] Because at the high end of the technological spectrum—for example, systems integration of high-performance fighter jets—there are still a relatively small number of producers, the natural difficulties of developing and enforcing a cooperative arrangement will be less.[104]

Joint Production of Armaments

To cope with reduced domestic demand for armaments without having a negative impact on domestic economies, defense producers probably will have to adopt fundamental restructuring of how they provide for their security. Joint production of weapons is the likely solution. Transnational cooperation is increasingly viewed by a number of governments to be the only affordable way to maintain a "critical minimum" of R&D and production capability. Such cooperation is a means of achieving economies of scale and gaining access to new markets, thereby helping to preserve the reduced levels of indigenous defense production.[105] As a consequence, a clear trend emerged among the western Europeans and Americans before the end of the cold war to move arms collaboration further back to the beginnings of the product cycle.[106] Multilateral cooperation offers participating nations a number of big incentives:

—Sharing of costs and reducing risks of researching, developing, and manufacturing new weapons systems.

—Gaining access to innovative foreign technologies.

—Helping to achieve economies of scale in the production of increasingly expensive weapon systems.

—Developing and penetrating foreign markets that might otherwise be closed to arms imports.

—Enhancing the combat efficiency and effectiveness of military alliances by eliminating wasteful duplication in arms production while promoting battlefield rationalization, standardization, and interoperability.

—Fostering other types of international cooperation, such as NATO political solidarity or west European economic integration.[107]

Although the notion of joint production of virtually all military armaments may seem radical, it would be both economically sensible and would foster the larger process of multilateral security cooperation in a world in which the United States, Russia, and other major military powers have reduced their military forces to levels sufficient only for defense or multilateral cooperative interventions. Representatives of Russian industry are very enthusiastic about joint development and production of weapons systems. The barriers exist largely at the government level and in U.S. industry. The west European states already participate in joint productions. The United States and Russia could join them.

Conclusion

The United States and Russia stand at a critical threshold. The relative harmony that has characterized their recent relations is increasingly threatened by the tendency of both countries to approach their short-term security interests independently. Most profoundly, efforts by both states to pursue expanded exports of weapons threaten to renew the competitive aspects of their bilateral relationship. Furthermore, myopic pursuit of increased arms exports will aggravate the security problems for each around the globe.

Ironically, increased competition and its attendant risks fly in the face of fundamental changes that are occurring in the global security, technological, and economic environments. These changes require that the traditional formula for provision of security in the United States and Russia be reworked. In particular, the retention of a large, isolated defense industrial base in each country poses a number of problems: It fails to provide the armed forces with cutting-edge technologies; it is a sizable economic burden; and its maintenance provides constant pressure for dangerous arms technology proliferation. If Russia continues to adhere to this faulty strategy, it courts continued economic crisis and, perhaps as a consequence, domestic political disruption and the failure of Russian reforms.

A cooperative approach by the United States and Russia is required for the rationalization and conversion of their defense sectors. Both states must adopt policies of restraint in arms sales in the near term, while cooperating in their efforts to convert excess defense industrial capacities to civilian tasks. In the long term, both states should consider options such as developing a new multilateral proliferation control regime and, perhaps, adopting a globalized approach to arms production. None of these tasks can be realized by either government acting independently; success requires cooperative management. Although obstacles to cooperation exist between the former adversaries, the logic of and returns from cooperation are much more profound.

Appendix

As an example of how the RAPID program could work, an American corporation (AmCo) would select a Russian enterprise (RusCo) as its partner for a RAPID project.[108] The two companies would identify one or more of AmCo's civilian products for manufacture and sale primarily in Russia through their joint venture. A business plan would be developed to lay out all elements for implementing the project, including details of the capital equipment, tooling, dollar working capital, preproduction supply of finished goods, components, know-how, and technical and management assistance to be furnished by AmCo.

The project would be carried out through a new corporation (NewRusCo) organized for the purpose, with its own board of directors and management. RusCo would contribute as much of its plant, equipment, working capital, and other assets as are to be used in the project to NewRusCo in exchange for NewRusCo shares. In each case, the number of NewRusCo shares to be issued would be based on the net value of the assets contributed. If AmCo is to contribute assets with a net value of $60 million and RusCo is to contribute net assets worth $40 million (the dollar value of the Russian assets), then AmCo would receive 60 percent and RusCo would receive 40 percent of NewRusCo's stock. Because NewRusCo would be a domestic Russian company, its shares would be denominated in rubles.

RusCo would also make available management and other personnel to become employees of NewRusCo. AmCo might also make personnel available to NewRusCo, either to be employed or serve as advisers. In any case, AmCo would enter into a five-year contract with NewRusCo to provide technical, management, and training assistance.

AmCo and RusCo would apply to RAPID for approval of the project. If approved, AmCo would be entitled to sell up to 90 percent of its NewRusCo shares to RAPID and receive cash payment in U.S. dollars. AmCo would retain at least 10 percent of the NewRusCo shares. RusCo could make

43

10 percent or more of its shares of NewRusCo available for purchase by Russians in exchange for privatization vouchers. NewRusCo would also be encouraged to establish equity ownership programs for its management and other employees, in the form of stock options or employee stock ownership plans.

RAPID would place all shares that it purchases from approved projects in an investment fund. The fund would raise cash to buy NewRusCo and other project shares by selling U.S. dollar-denominated shares of the fund through underwriters to private U.S. and other investors. The full amount of equity investment in the RAPID fund would be guaranteed jointly by the U.S. and Russian governments after five years. The guaranty would expire at the end of ten years. The Russian government would also guarantee the convertibility of any ruble proceeds from sale of Russian shares held by the fund, so that the fund would be able to repatriate the share values for its investors in U.S. dollars.

As a result of this process, when NewRusCo launches its business, its stock would be owned by RusCo, Russian private investors (through privatization vouchers), the RAPID fund, and AmCo. Subsequently, NewRusCo could sell additional shares of its stock to raise additional capital. Such shares could be sold through public offerings to Russian or other investors, or by private placements. The development of the public market for NewRusCo stock should be encouraged.

Notes

1. Predictions of future market growth reflect three factors: (1) residual deliveries of primarily Western systems purchased in the aftermath of the Gulf War; (2) modestly increasing deliveries to the Gulf States, Iran, and, eventually, Iraq; and (3) a 3 to 5 percent annual increase in the value of deliveries to Asian countries. See William J. Durch and Steven M. Irwin with Jonathan Henick, "The International Arms Market: Variables Affecting Russian Sales Prospects," paper prepared for the International Arms Sales Conference held by the Brookings Institution and the Institute for USA and Canada Studies, Queenstown, Md., February 3–5, 1994, p. 14.

2. Value is a constant U.S. dollar figure that facilitates the comparison of the level or size of a country's arms exports across time or with other states. These calculations are based on Stockholm International Peace Research Institute (SIPRI) data in constant dollars. See Randall Forsberg and Jonathan Cohen, "The Global Arms Market: Prospects for the Coming Decade," paper prepared for the International Arms Sales Conference held by the Brookings Institution and the Institute for USA and Canada Studies, Queenstown, Md., February 3–5, 1994, table 1.1.

Richard F. Grimmett of the Congressional Research Service found a similar decline using a different methodology. The value of all deliveries in global arms exports to the Third World declined in real terms by 60 percent between 1986 and 1993. The 1993 value of arms deliveries to the Third World had the lowest yearly total (in both nominal and real terms) by a substantial margin for any year during the 1986–93 period. See Richard F. Grimmett, *Conventional Arms Transfers to the Third World, 1986–93*, CRS Report to Congress (Congressional Research Service, July 29, 1994), table 2 and p. 5.

3. Forsberg and Cohen, *The Global Arms Market*, figure 6.

4. Russia's reported exports of military equipment worth $4.5 billion in 1993 represented an almost 30 percent increase over the 1992 level. See *SIPRI Yearbook 1994* (Oxford University Press, 1994), table 13.8, p. 484.

5. For example, in exchange for the MiG-29 combat aircraft sent to Malaysia,

Moscow will accept one-quarter of the payment in the form of palm oil. Export agreements with India similarly allow for payment to Moscow in the form of tea and rupees. See Sergey Mashtakov, "MiG - i v Malayzii. Kto eshche kupit nashi istrebiteli?" ("MiG" also in Malaysia. Who else will buy our fighters?) *Rossiyskaya Gazeta*, September 7, 1994, p. 3; and "Shibayev, Deputy Chairman of the Committee for Foreign Economic Relations: If Everyone Were Allowed to Sell Arms, the Unjustified Competition Would Lead to a Fall in Prices," *Komsomolskaya Pravda*, February 25, 1992, p. 1, translated in *Foreign Broadcast Information Service—Central Eurasia*, 92-039, pp. 31–32. (Hereafter, *FBIS-SOV*.)

6. The Russian government has adopted a wide-scale approach to using excess—or even newly procured—weapons to pay off its foreign debts. See S. Tsekhmistrenko, "Monopolist mostit dorogu na rynok blagimi namereniyami" (Monopolist paves the road to the market with good intentions), *Kommersant-Daily*, March 24, 1994, p. 4.

7. See John Lepingwell, "German-Russian and EU Trade Discussed," *RFE-RL Daily Report*, May 13, 1994; and Jiri Pehe, "Czech Republic, Russia Agree on Deb Payments," *RFE/RL Daily Report*, April 6, 1994.

8. Durch and Irwin with Henick, "The International Arms Market," p. 16. For an analysis of the Middle East upgrade market, see Philip Finnegan, "Middle East Focus Shifts to Upgrades," *Defense News*, March 14–20, 1994, p. 12.

9. For example, Korean Air and Bristol Aerospace of Canada have teamed to offer upgrade packages for the nearly two thousand F-5 fighters in service around the world, while companies from Israel and Romania have teamed to compete with the Russians for providing upgrades for the MiG-21. See Durch and Irwin with Henick, "The International Arms Market," p. 16.

10. The U.S. Air Force hopes to use revenues from sales of its used redundant aircraft to finance its future development projects. Similarly, President Boris N. Yeltsin in 1992 gave permission to the Russian Air Force High Command to sell off sixteen hundred redundant fighters despite the aerospace industry's efforts to sell new systems. See Gilbert A. Lewthwaite, "Pentagon Weighs Sale of Arms to Earn Billions," *Baltimore Sun*, March 16, 1994, p. 1; and M. Polyakov and A. Kovalev, "Plus Eleven," Moscow Television, May 2, 1992, translated in *FBIS-SOV*, 92-092, pp. 14–15.

11. "Glut of Surplus Defense Equipment Draws Congressional Attention," *Aerospace Daily*, August 13, 1993, p. 262; "Contractors Seek to Curb Low-Cost Sales," *Jane's Defence Weekly*, August 14, 1993, p. 13; and cited in Durch and Irwin with Henick, "The International Arms Market," p. 15.

12. During the 1980–87 period, offsets provided by U.S. firms totaled approximately 57 percent of the value of U.S. arms sales. Given the increasingly competitive market, the level of offsets is sure to increase. For example, offsets for the anticipated Israeli purchase of F-16s or F/A-18s are estimated at nearly 80 percent. See Durch and Irwin with Henick, "The International Arms Market," p. 20.

13. Durch and Irwin with Henick, "The International Arms Market," p. 29.

14. Tsekhmistrenko, "Monopolist mostit dorogu na rynok blagimi namereniyami," p. 4.

15. Estimates of future arms export earnings by Russian government officials range from $9 billion to $20 billion per year. See the comments of the chairman of Rosvooruzheniye, Viktor Samoylov, in Keith Bush, "An Optimistic Projection of Arms Sales," *RFE-RL Daily Report,* March 31, 1994; the comments of Mikhail Maley, in Laszlo Vida, "Only the Military-Industrial Complex Can Ensure the Continuation of the Reforms, Mikhail Maley, A Chief Lobbyist of the 'Oboronka' Says," *Magyar Nemzet,* December 30, 1993, p. 2, translated in *FBIS-SOV,* 94-003, pp. 44–45; and the comments of Minister of the Economy Aleksandr Shokhin, cited in Keith Bush, "Projection of Arms Exports," *RFE-RL Daily Report,* December 1, 1993.

16. Soviet arms export policymaking had become so politicized and disaggregated, several former officials conceded that they had had no idea of the real size of Soviet arms exports. See the comments of former foreign ministers Eduard Shevardnadze and Aleksandr Bessmertnykh, in Petr Vasilyev, "Buy an Aircraft Carrier," *Novoye Vremya,* no. 17 (April 1993), pp. 18–21, translated in *Joint Publications Research Service—Central Eurasia Military Affairs,* 93-023, pp. 38–42.

17. Economist Clifford G. Gaddy argued that, throughout the 1980s, the Soviet government received less than $3 billion annually in hard currency. This reflected an assumption that only 25 percent of its transactions were for cash and only 50–60 percent of the credit was repaid. See Clifford G. Gaddy, *Civilianizing Russia: How Factories and Families Are Adjusting to Life in a Nonmilitarized Economy* (Brookings, forthcoming). For a Russian estimate of cash transactions amounting to one-third of all arms deliveries between 1986 and 1990, see Pavel Fel'gengauer, "Rezkoye sokrashcheniye eksporta otechestvennogo oruzhiya vpervyye obyavleny ofitsial'nyye tsifry voyenno tekhnicheskogo sotrudnichestva za 1991 god" (Sharp reduction in exports of our weapons: the first releases of official figures of military-technical cooperation for 1991), *Nezavisimaya Gazeta,* September 29, 1992, pp. 1–2. See also the comments of Samoylov, in Bush, "An Optimistic Projection of Arms Sales"; and Marshal of Aviation Yevgeniy Shaposhnikov, "Ot Razumnoy dostatochnosti k dostatochnoy razumnosti" (From reasonable sufficiency to sufficient reasonableness), *Izvestiya,* May 12, 1994, p. 5.

18. On the problems of conversion and the survival of the Russian defense industries in general, see Kevin P. O'Prey, *Converting and Restructuring the Russian Defense Industries: The Need for a Strategic Partnership* (New York: Twentieth Century Fund, forthcoming).

19. Gennadiy Yanpolskiy of the State Committee for the Defense Branches of Industry argued that, although armaments account for only 25 percent of the output in Russia's defense sector, they account for 75 percent of its export revenues. See Igor Chernyak, "VPK: Gruzite tanki samoletami. Vernet li Rossiya milliardy dollarov ot eksporta oruzhiya?" (MIC: load tanks with aircraft. Will Russia get back billions of dollars from the export of weapons?), *Komsomolskaya Pravda,* February 1, 1994, p. 2.

20. On the efforts to reduce political pressure for subsidies to industry, see Clifford G. Gaddy and Melanie L. Allen, *Russian Arms Sales Abroad: Policy, Practice, and Prospects,* Brookings Discussion Paper, September 1993, p. 55; and

Andrey A. Kokoshin, "Defense Industry Conversion in the Russian Federation," in Teresa Pelton Johnson and Steven E. Miller, eds., *Russian Security after the Cold War: Seven Views from Moscow* (Brasseys, US, 1994), p. 60. On providing enterprises with financing for their conversion efforts, see comments of President Yeltsin in *Itar-TASS*, 1532 GMT, November 16, 1993, reprinted in *FBIS-SOV*, 93–220, p. 60. See also Prime Minister Viktor Chernomyrdin's preface to the defense industry journal, "Voyenny Parad" (Military parade), cited in Vladimir Gondusov, *Itar-TASS*, 2112 GMT, February 8, 1994, reprinted in *FBIS-SOV*, 94–027, pp. 24–25.

21. Defense-related employment in the United States is declining at a rate of twenty thousand jobs per month. Such employment has fallen 20 percent since 1987, including an 11 percent drop in 1993 alone. See Jeff Cole and Sarah Lubman, "Weapons Merchants Are Going Great Guns in Post–Cold War Era," *Wall Street Journal*, January 28, 1994, pp. A1, A6. In Russia, the republic of Udmurtiya is especially sensitive to the decline in defense procurement. In recent years 57 percent of its labor and perhaps 85 percent of its industrial output has been in the defense sector. See Brenda Horrigan, "How Many People Worked in Soviet Defense Industry?" *RFE/RL Research Report*, August 21, 1992, pp. 33–39; and Gaddy and Allen, *Russian Arms Sales Abroad*.

22. Two examples are the new Kamov attack helicopter, Ka-50, and the new Sukhoi fighter-bomber, the Su-30. See, for example, Stephen Foye, "Military Cooperation Advanced," *RFE-RL Daily Report*, July 1, 1994.

23. See Janne E. Nolan and others, "The Imperatives for Cooperation," in Janne E. Nolan, ed., *Global Engagement: Cooperation and Security in the 21st Century* (Brookings, 1994), p. 27.

24. Russia and Ukraine, for example, both have sold tanks to Iran. Russia has also transferred submarines to Iran and North Korea. This has caused considerable consternation in U.S. efforts to create a new, post–CoCom multilateral export control regime. CoCom is the seventeen-nation Coordinating Committee on Multilateral Export Controls. See Mary Mycio and Sonni Efron, "Ukraine Will Try to Revive Arms Industry, Lawmakers Say," *Los Angeles Times* (Washington edition), July 13, 1994, p. 2; and Stephen Foye, "Problems with CoCom," *RFE-RL Daily Report*, April 8, 1994.

25. Comments of a Russian participant, *Transcript of Reports and Discussion*, prepared for the International Arms Sales Conference held by the Brookings Institution and the Institute of USA and Canada, Queenstown, Md., February 3–5, 1994; and Igor Khripunov, "Russia"s Arms Trade in the Post–Cold War Period," *Washington Quarterly*, vol. 17 (Autumn 1994), pp. 86–87.

26. Although in 1983 the shares of the world arms market held by the United States and USSR were roughly equal (32 percent each), their fortunes diverged thereafter. By 1992 the United States controlled 46 percent of the market, while Russia's share had dropped to 11 percent. See Forsberg and Cohen, *The Global Arms Market*, table 1.1; and Yelena Belova, "Oboronnyy zakaz v 1994 godu sokrashchen ne budet. Torgovlya noveyshim oruzhiyem vygodnee konversii, schitayut oboronshchiki" (Defense orders will not be cut in 1994. Trade in the most modern weapons is more profitable than conversion, the defense community believes), *Segodnya*, December 25, 1993, p. 2.

27. This view has adherents in the Russian government and legislature. See, for example, the comments of Chairman of the Federation Council Vladimir Shumeiko, in John Lepingwell, "Shumeiko on Partnership for Peace," *RFE-RL Daily Report*, June 15, 1994.

28. See, for example, the critical comments of Foreign Minister Andrey Kozyrev as cited in Stephen Foye, "Kozyrev on Arms Sales, Karabakh," *RFE-RL Daily Report*, June 1, 1994.

29. As cited in Durch and Irwin with Henick, "The International Arms Market," p. 29.

30. See Randall Forsberg, ed., *The Arms Production Dilemma* (MIT Press, 1994), appendix, p. 295. Another estimate puts the current level of overcapacity in the U.S. defense aerospace industry at 50-60 percent. See Anthony L. Velocci, Jr., "Northrop, Martin Battle for Grumman," *Aviation Week and Space Technology*, March 14, 1994, p. 27; and John D. Morocco, "Arms Modernization Key Long-Term Goal," *Aviation Week and Space Technology*, March 14, 1994, p. 48.

31. Keith Bush, "Decline of Defense Industry Decried," *RFE-RL Daily Report*, April 28, 1994.

32. See *Interfax* report cited in Stephen Foye, "Russian Airforce to Cut Aircraft, Modernize," *RFE-RL Daily Report*, April 14, 1994.

33. Forsberg, *The Arms Production Dilemma*, appendix, p. 293.

34. See Giovanni de Briganti, "European Missile Makers Continue Consolidation Pattern," *Defense News*, June 21, 1993, cited in Richard A. Bitzinger, *The Globalization of Arms Production: Defense Markets in Transition* (Washington: Defense Budget Project, 1993).

35. See John D. Steinbruner, "Weapons Production and Force Structure Planning as a Problem of Collaboration," paper prepared for the International Arms Sales Conference held by the Brookings Institution and the Institute for USA and Canada Studies, Queenstown, Md., February 3–5, 1994, p. 2; and Ashton B. Carter, William J. Perry, and John D. Steinbruner, *A New Concept of Cooperative Security*, Brookings Occasional Papers, (Brookings, 1992), p. 2.

36. During the Persian Gulf War, the coalition forces effectively employed stealth technologies and precision-guided munitions to suppress Iraqi defenses. For example, Tomahawk cruise missiles and F-117 fighters equipped with laser-guided weapons helped reduce coalition attrition of aircraft to remarkably small rates. See Carter, Perry, and Steinbruner, *A New Concept of Cooperative Security*, pp. 29–30.

37. See, for example, the comments of Dorothy Robyn, special assistant to the president for economic policy, who complained that the Department of Defense does not have first access to cutting-edge technologies. She argued that advances in technology in areas such as electronics are emerging in the commercial sector, where company accounting practices are often incompatible with Department of Defense standards. See "DOD Acquisition Reform Plan Heading to Perry," *Aerospace Daily*, February 24, 1994, p. 293; and Jacques S. Gansler, "Constructively Managing Russian Defense Industry Downsizing," paper prepared for the International Arms Sales Conference held by the Brookings Institution and the Institute for USA and Canada Studies, Queenstown, Md., February 3–5, 1994, p. 3.

38. At the same time that the electronics content of modern weapons is increasing, many of the components used in defense-electronic systems and subsystems can be obtained commercially at much lower cost. The demand for military-specific items is contracting, thereby pressuring component suppliers who cannot compete with commercial producers. See Anthony L. Velocci, Jr., "Consolidation Outlook Stormy," *Aviation Week and Space Technology*, March 14, 1994, p. 44; and Gansler, "Constructively Managing Russian Defense Industry Downsizing," p. 6.

39. See First Deputy Minister of Defense Andrey A. Kokoshin, "Protivorechiya formirovaniya i puti razvitiya voenno-tekhnicheskoy politiki Rossiy" (Contradictions of formation and ways of developing the military-technical policy of Russia), *Voennaya Mysl'*, no. 2 (1993).

40. The difference in success rates is attributable to the substantial difference between defense and commercial businesses. See Jacques S. Gansler, "Constructively Transforming the Russian Defense Industry," February 28, 1994, p. 9.

41. See, for example, David Bernstein, "Conversion," in Michael McFaul, ed., *Can the Russian Military-Industrial Complex Be Privatized? Evaluating the Experiment in Employee Ownership at the Saratov Aviation Plant* (Stanford University, Center for International Security and Arms Control, 1993), p. 7; and Arthur J. Alexander, "Perspectives on Russian Defense Industry Conversion," *Business in the Contemporary World* (Autumn 1993), p. 64.

42. Remarks of an American participant, *Transcript of Reports and Discussions*.

43. Gansler, "Constructively Transforming the Russian Defense Industry," p. 16.

44. Gansler, "Constructively Transforming the Russian Defense Industry," p. 17.

45. Gansler, "Constructively Transforming the Russian Defense Industry," pp. 16–17.

46. Gansler, "Constructively Transforming the Russian Defense Industry," p. 16.

47. For an executive branch argument on the need to reduce the "ghettoization" of the U.S. defense industrial base, see the comments of Robyn, in "DOD Acquisition Reform Plan Heading to Perry."

For a review of the current state of integration between U.S. defense and commercial sectors and prospects for the future, see U.S. Congress, Office of Technology Assessment, *Assessing the Potential for Civil-Military Technology, Processes, and Practices*, OTA-ISS-611 (Washington, D.C., U.S. Government Printing Office, September 1994.

48. Jacques S. Gansler, "Defense Conversion: Transforming the U.S. Defense Industrial Base," *Survival* (Winter 1993–94), pp. 130–46.

49. See Gansler, "Constructively Transforming the Russian Defense Industry," p. 12.

50. Gansler, "Constructively Transforming the Russian Defense Industry."

51. See Nolan and others, "The Imperatives for Cooperation," p. 29.

52. Gansler, "Constructively Transforming the Russian Defense Industry," pp. 12–13.

53. See Bitzinger, *The Globalization of Arms Production*, pp. 8–15.

54. See the comments of Robyn, in "DOD Acquisition Reform Plan Heading to Perry."

55. A number of empirical studies have highlighted the aversion of heavily defense-dependent firms to diversification. See, for example, Richard A. Bitzinger, *Adjusting to the Drawdown: The Transition in the Defense Industry* (Washington: Defense Budget Project, April 1993); and James B. Steinberg, *The Transformation of the European Defense Industry* (Santa Monica, Calif.: RAND Corporation, 1992), pp. 65–67.

56. Much of the following section is based on the insightful comments of a conference participant from the U.S. aerospace industry, *Transcript of Reports and Discussion.*

57. See comments of a U.S. aerospace industry participant, *Transcript of Reports and Discussion*; and Richard A. Bitzinger, "Customize Defense Industry Restructuring," *Orbis* (Spring 1994), pp. 267–71.

58. These assets are the Electric Boat Division (submarines) and the Michigan tank production facility.

59. When a defense firms sells technology or process to another company, government auditors will demand that the defense producer reduce the cost of the original defense product because of the broadening of the overhead base. In general, this is less often the case for defense firms that possess their own commercial subsidiary that can sell technologies to another company. See comments of an American participant, *Transcript of Reports and Discussion.*

60. Raytheon has been expanding its nondefense interests by purchasing assets of a construction company and British Aerospace PLC's business jet unit. The company aims to have half of its earnings come from commercial ventures. The defense side accounted for 65 percent of its earnings in 1994. See Steve Stecklow, "Raytheon Plans to Consolidate, Cut 4,400 Jobs," *Wall Street Journal*, March 10, 1994, p. 3.

61. A January 1993 U.S. Central Intelligence Agency study estimated the number of defense enterprises in the Russian Federation to be between two thousand and four thousand. See CIA Directorate of Intelligence, *The Defense Industries of the Newly Independent States of Eurasia*, OSE 93-10001, January 1993, p. 5. According to the Russian State Committee for the Management of State Property, there are two thousand defense enterprises. See Keith Bush, "Most Defense Enterprises to Be Privatized by End 1994," *RFE-RL Daily Report*, March 1, 1994.

62. According to Russian sources, USSR/Russian arms procurement orders dropped 50 percent during the 1990–91 period and another 67 percent during 1992. The procurement budget has been held steady since then. See Irina Lapina, interview with Deputy Premier Georgiy Khizha, "How Will We Live?," Russian Television Network, 0815 GMT, September 12, 1992, translated in *FBIS-SOV*, 92–186, pp. 25–35; and Belova, "Oboronnyy zakaz v 1994 godu sokrashchen ne budet."

63. For example, the U.S. Defense Intelligence Agency estimated that Russia failed to produce a single attack helicopter in 1992 and only ten in 1993. See William Grundman, director for combat support, Defense Intelligence Agency, "Statement for the Record," to the Joint Economic Committee, 103d Cong. 2 sess. (July 15, 1994), table 1.

64. Kevin P. O'Prey, "Observations on Adaptation, Restructuring, and Conversion in Russian Defense Enterprises and Regional Government," June 1994.

65. The Russian Law on Defense called for a reduction in the size of Russian armed forces so that no more than 1 percent of the population is under arms—roughly 1.5 million troops—by January 1995. See John Leppingwell, "Restructuring the Russian Military," *RFE/RL Research Report*, June 18, 1993, p. 19. On the industrial side, the ministry is focusing its scarce orders on a small number of producers that it considers to be vital. For example, the ministry has limited its orders for tanks and submarines to only one producer in each of those sectors. See Kokoshin, "Protivorechiya formirovaniya i puti razvitiya voenno-tekhnicheskoy politiki Rossiy."

66. The 1994 Russian defense budget was approximately $30 billion. Full financing of a 1.5 million Russian military under the most favorable of assumptions would require approximately $94.6 billion. See Steinbruner, "Weapons Production and Force Structure Planning as a Problem of Collaboration," pp. 13–14 and table 6.

67. See the comments of Viktor Glukhikh in "Business in Russia," Russian Television Network, 1300 GMT, September 27, 1993, translated in *FBIS-SOV*, 93–192, p. 12.

68. O'Prey, *Converting and Restructuring the Russian Defense Industries.*

69. Most Russian defense enterprises are scheduled to be privatized by the end of 1994. See Bush, "Most Defense Enterprises to Be Privatized by End 1994."

70. O'Prey, *Converting and Restructuring the Russian Defense Industries.*

71. See Nolan and others, "The Imperatives for Cooperation," p. 51.

72. On the need for such controls, see Sergey Kortunov, "National Export Control System for Russia," *Comparative Strategy*, vol. 13 (January–March 1994), pp. 231–38.

73. An international first step in this direction has already been taken with the creation of the United Nations Register of Conventional Arms. See Malcom Chalmers and Owen Greene, "Developing International Transparency: Successes for the United Nations Register of Conventional Arms," *International Defense Review*, vol. 5 (1994), pp. 23–27; and Herbert Wulf, "The United Nations Register of Conventional Arms," in *SIPRI Yearbook 1993: World Armaments and Disarmament* (Oxford University Press, 1993), pp. 533–44.

74. Alternatively, if this option is too difficult politically, governments should at least identify the firms, enterprises, or capabilities that are clearly not a priority.

75. The latter appears to be the strategy, for example, of Pratt and Whitney in its collaboration with Ilyushin on the new Ilyushin-96M commercial airliner. Encountering problems of reduced demand for jet engines in the West, Pratt and Whitney evidently hopes to find new markets by supplying the engines for the Russian air transport, which Ilyushin hopes to export. Double Cola, a recipient of Nunn-Lugar support for its joint venture with the Russian enterprise NPO Mashinostroyeniya, similarly is setting up a production and bottling facility to sell soda in Russia. See White House, Office of the Vice President, U.S.-Russian Joint Commission on Economic and Technological Cooperation, "Report of the Defense Conversion Committee," press release, June 23, 1994.

76. The Russian partners—the Khrunichev Space Center and the Scientific Production Association Energiya—formed a joint company with Lockheed in early 1993. See "Launch of Satellite Joint Venture in Russia Works, Lockheed Says," *Journal of Commerce*, March 21, 1993, p. 3b; and Louise Kahoe, "Satellite Venture Wins $600m Contracts," *London Financial Times*, March 18, 1994, p. 1.

77. Much of the argument here is shared in Fund for Democracy and Development. See The Fund for Democracy and Development, *A New Strategy for United States Assistance to Russia and the Newly Independent States*, A Report of the Fund's Policy Panel (January 10, 1994).

78. In public auctions of company shares thus far, even Russian investors appear reluctant to invest in defense plants because they fear that the state will restrict the flexibility of the plant management. See Alexander Kovalev and Sergei Chikker, "Defense, Engineering Plants Go for a Song," *Commersant*, October 6, 1993, pp. 13–14.

79. The creation of small enterprises (malyye predpriyatiya) spin-offs from within the structure of old enterprises is still a somewhat controversial process in legal terms. In many cases, the director of a profitable department of an enterprise opts to privatize his department and separate from the larger organization. Not surprisingly, the director of the larger enterprise often objects to this maneuver, unless he is a partner in the new firm. The extended jurisdictional fights over these matters often involve different branches of the government and serve to delay the process of industrial restructuring. On spin-offs in Russia generally, see David Bernstein, "Spin-Offs and Start-Ups in Russia: A Key Element of Industrial Restructuring," in Michael McFaul and Tova Perlmutter, eds., *Privatization, Conversion, and Enterprise Reform in Russia*, (Stanford University, Center for International Security and Arms Control, May 1994), pp. 201–15.

80. The January 1994 Law on Privatization legally permits a degree of foreign ownership, but whether it is permitted in reality remains to be seen. See "Gosudarstvennaya programa privatizatsiy gosudarstvennykh i munitsipal'nykh predpriyatiy v Rossiyskoy Federatsii" (State program of privatization of state and municipal enterprises in the Russian Federation), *Rossiyskiye Vesti*, January 5, 1994, pp. 3–7.

81. The Overseas Private Investment Corporation (OPIC) provides direct loans to small and medium-size companies to fulfill up to 50 percent of the total project cost for a new venture and up to 75 percent of the total cost of an expansion. OPIC also provides investment insurance in developing countries to account for political risks such as political violence affecting assets or business income, expropriation without fair compensation, and inconvertibility of currency. The Clinton administration has already used OPIC effectively to encourage private investment in the former Soviet Union. For example, it has granted OPIC with $1 billion of authority over the 1994–95 period for project finance in the region. See "Overseas Private Investment Corporation (OPIC)," Department of Commerce FlashFax service, February 11, 1994.

82. See Section 1207 of the National Defense Authorization of FY 1994, P.L. 103-160, and the Department of Defense Appropriations Act of 1994, P.L. 103-109.

83. Since 1991 the U.S. Congress has authorized that $1.2 billion of the Defense Department's budget be applied to specified Nunn-Lugar tasks.

84. See Theodor Galdi, *The Nunn-Lugar Cooperative Threat Reduction Program for Soviet Weapons Dismantlement: Background and Implementation*, CRS Report to Congress (Congressional Research Service Report, December 29, 1993).

85. The four enterprises are the State Scientific Research Institute for Avionics Systems (GosNIIAS) in Moscow; the Scientific Production Association (NPO) Mashinostroyeniya and the Istok Research and Production Corporation, both in the Moscow region; and the Leninets Holding Company in St. Petersburg.

86. See, for example, Office of the Assistant Secretary of Defense (Public Affairs), "SecDef Announces Defense Conversion Contract Awards," press release, June 23, 1994.

87. For example, the U.S. government is providing $1.9 million to a project valued at $3.9 million that joins International American Products of Columbia, South Carolina, with the Leninets Holding Company for the production of dental chairs and equipment. See Office of the Assistant Secretary of Defense (Public Affairs), "SecDef Announces Defense Conversion Contract Awards."

88. The five enterprises are NPO Kompozit, NPO Mashinostroyeniya, NPO Soyuz, Mil Design Bureau and Production plant, and Energomash. See "Funds for Russian Defense Conversion," Department of Commerce Flashfax service, February 2, 1994; and Tom McCabe, Defense Nuclear Agency contracting officer, remarks to Site-Visit Conference, Moscow, April 12, 1994.

89. See Office of the Assistant Secretary of Defense (Public Affairs), "DOD Announces Defense Enterprise Fund Grant," press release, June 23, 1994. The fund has been authorized up to $40 million, although only $7.67 million has been obligated.

90. First, the Department of Defense had to identify which of its own programs would sacrifice part of their budget to provide the resources. Then the Department of Defense comptroller would seek approval from the House and Senate Appropriations committees for the specific projects and their sources of financing. See Galdi, *The Nunn-Lugar Cooperative Threat Reduction Program for Soviet Weapons Dismantlement*, p. 9.

91. The participation of American suppliers would also include a five-year technical and management assistance agreement for installation, training, production, product improvement, quality, marketing, sales, distribution, accounting, and finance. The goal would be not only to facilitate the operation of the new production facilities, but also to improve the management of the entity as a business venture. See Committee on Enterprise Management in a Market Economy under Defense Conversion, *A Russian-American Partnership for Industrial Development (RAPID)* (Washington: National Academy Press, 1993), p. 5.

92. These early projects would then provide a real portfolio for an initial public offering of the RAPID equity shares. Committee on Enterprise Management in a Market Economy under Defense Conversion, *A Russian-American Partnership for Industrial Development*, p. 6.

93. If the fund were to fail and the Russian government lacked adequate currency,

it could fulfill its obligation by transferring to the U.S. government ownership of extracted natural resources or offsets against U.S. government payments committed to Russia (such as funds to be transferred in exchange for Russian uranium). See Committee on Enterprise Management in a Market Economy under Defense Conversion, *A Russian-American Partnership for Industrial Development*, pp. 5–6.

94. Even in the case of the fund's failure, the budgetary cash costs for the U.S. and Russian governments would not equal the total amount guaranteed by RAPID. Because the fund would sell shares of the Russian joint ventures to cover all or part of the guaranty, the U.S. and Russian governments would have to pay only the differences between the amount guaranteed by the fund and the amount actually raised by selling the joint venture shares. See Committee on Enterprise Management in a Market Economy under Defense Conversion, *A Russian-American Partnership for Industrial Development*, pp. 6–7.

95. See Kortunov, "National Export Control System for Russia."

96. Indeed, one of the Fast Four projects teams a U.S. firm—Rockwell-Collins—with a Russian avionics institute to develop air traffic control systems.

97. See Nolan and others, "The Imperatives for Cooperation," p. 53. On the limitations of cartel or denial arrangements in the current international environment, see also Wolfgang H. Reinicke, "Cooperative Security and the Political Economy of Nonproliferation," in Nolan, *Global Engagement*, p. 179.

98. Janne E. Nolan and John D. Steinbruner, "A Transition Strategy for the 1990s," in Nolan, *Global Engagement*, p. 580.

99. The U.N. General Assembly has already taken a limited step in this direction. In December 1991 it passed a resolution to establish a system of voluntary registration of all arms exports and imports. See Nolan and Steinbruner, "A Transition Strategy for the 1990s," p. 580. Such transparency regimes are already widespread in the world of commerce. Securities markets, for example, depend on the transparency established by the National Association of Securities Dealers (NASD). The National Association of Securities Dealers Automated Quotation (NASDAQ) system is a computerized system that provides price information on the stocks of thousands of companies to broker-dealers. NASDAQ monitors the system to watch for unusual price and volume movements that might indicate unlawful activity. See Reinicke, "Cooperative Security and the Political Economy of Nonproliferation," pp. 186–87.

100. This should not be confused with deregulation. On the contrary, this would be a more realistic and practical form of regulation. Reinicke, "Cooperative Security and the Political Economy of Nonproliferation," pp. 179, 181.

101. Reinicke, "Cooperative Security and the Political Economy of Nonproliferation," pp. 187–88.

102. Nolan and Steinbruner, "A Transition Strategy for the 1990s," p. 580.

103. See Reinicke, "Cooperative Security and the Political Economy of Nonproliferation," p. 180 and n. 30.

104. Given the extant diffusion of technologies at the low end of the spectrum, too many producers already exist for a realistic chance of incorporating them all in a cooperative regime.

105. Bitzinger, *The Globalization of Arms Production*, pp. i–ii.

106. Ibid., p. 14.

107. Ibid., p. 5.

108. Example drawn from Committee on Enterprise Management in a Market Economy under Defense Conversion, *A Russian-American Partnership for Industrial Development*, pp. 6–9.

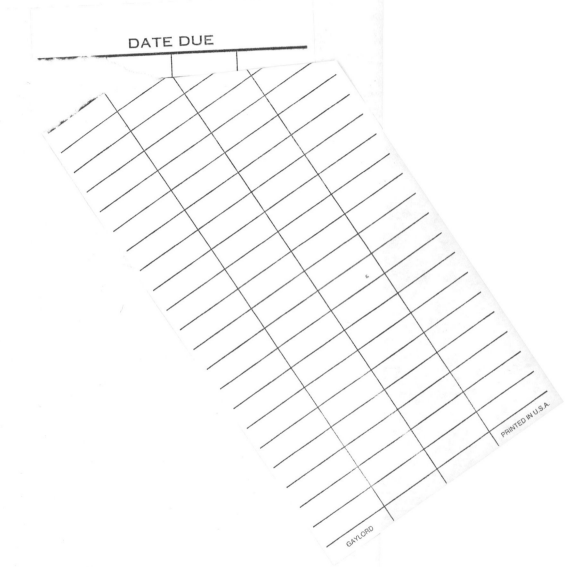

DATE DUE

GAYLORD

PRINTED IN U.S.A.